THE COUNTRYMAN'S ENGLAND

J. N. Turner

from H & T. S. Alexander.

The BRITISH HERITAGE Series
Uniform with this Volume 7s. 6d. net each

THE HEART OF ENGLAND
By IVOR BROWN

ENGLISH VILLAGES AND HAMLETS
By HUMPHREY PAKINGTON

THE OLD INNS OF ENGLAND
By A. E. RICHARDSON

THE PARISH CHURCHES OF ENGLAND
By J. CHARLES COX and C. BRADLEY FORD

THE CATHEDRALS OF ENGLAND
By HARRY BATSFORD and CHARLES FRY

THE SPIRIT OF LONDON
By PAUL COHEN-PORTHEIM

THE FACE OF SCOTLAND
By HARRY BATSFORD and CHARLES FRY

THE HEART OF SCOTLAND
By GEORGE BLAKE

Published by
B. T. BATSFORD LTD
15 North Audley Street, London, W.1

1 THRESHING

*From a Painting by John Nash in
the Collection of Lance Sieveking*

THE COUNTRYMAN'S ENGLAND

By

DOROTHY HARTLEY

With a Foreword by
A. G. STREET

LONDON
B. T. BATSFORD LTD
15 NORTH AUDLEY STREET, W.1

First Published, June 1935

MADE AND PRINTED IN GREAT BRITAIN
FOR THE PUBLISHERS, B. T. BATSFORD LTD., LONDON
TEXT BY UNWIN BROTHERS LTD., WOKING
PLATES BY THE DARIEN PRESS, EDINBURGH

CONTENTS

". . . But if the land fails?
Then fails meat and bread, for both rich and poor,
And all manner of men that by meat and drink labour.
Therefore, let all manner of men who by meat live
Help him to work vigorously who winneth our food.
'By Christ!' quoth a knight, 'he teaches us best
(And on this point truly taught was I never);
I myself would now assay some help, for solace as it were.'
'Truly, Sir Knight,' replied Piers the Plowman,
'I will work and sweat and sow for us both,
And labour as long as I live, all a lifetime,
If in return thou protect Holy Church and myself
From wasters and wicked men who would the earth destroy.'
'By my Power,' quoth the knight, 'I plight thee my troth
To fulfil this, though I fight shall
As long as I live . . .' "

LANGLAND's *Piers Plowman* ("A" Text)

2 CLOUDS AND SHEEP ON THE SOUTH DOWNS

3   THE REAN FURROW

THE COUNTRYMAN'S ENGLAND

CHAPTER I

INTRODUCTORY

HERE is no attempt to review the agricultural situation, nor comment upon the state of affairs in the English countryside. There are places in England to-day that cheer the heart with hopeful enterprise, and other places that are full of sorrow and disappointment. I know the impossibility of dealing in generalities, because in country England no two places are ever alike. The uniformity, that is automatic in the towns, is one of the most difficult attainments in the country. In every way this small island is extraordinarily varied. We have mountains, plains and marshes, and we register an "Average Equable Insular Climate," which (being interpreted) means we may freeze one minute and bake the next! I have left Snowdon in a blizzard of sleet and icy wind, and a few hours later have arrived wearing top boots and oilskins in a London heat wave.

Variety enforces adaptability, and the country usage varies as much as the climate imposed upon it. This makes classification schemes for a book of this kind very difficult. The present arrangement is necessarily imperfect; the boundaries of chapters and districts overlap in all directions, but the method of dividing according to the variety of the land is the simplest I can find, and if the divisions seem unusual, please believe that they are the result of much careful study, and have been approved in general by several geographical authorities.

Also, it is impossible for me to see country life and work with the detachment of an outsider—for I have spent all my life in the English countryside. I was born in Yorkshire (that austere, beautiful district called "The Dales"), and spent some of my happiest childhood in the cottage of my old nurse at Appletreewick. Among the sheep walks I learnt to twang a wool staple between my thumbs, long before I reluctantly learnt to read or write.

From Yorkshire I went to Oxfordshire and met real orchards, a wonder to a Northern lass who knew only the purple staining bilberry, and the wind-shuddered raspberry canes, in a cold world where even the gooseberries wore hairy coats. Going South to a sheltered garden sun-pool, I ate Moor Park apricocks, hot off a yellow Cotswold stone wall (and thought Paradise fruit could taste no sweeter!). Returning to a Coast-guard Station in the North of Scotland I carried back yellow bronzed pears, and blue downy plums, as gifts, but the bairns "could no' believe they were real fruities," and set them above the board, "to look at, no' to eat." From these friends in the North-West I got into a herring boat and first landed and explored the Western Islands; being snowed up during a terrible winter in a shepherd's hut, sharing warm hospitality with the dogs, the pony, whose stall adjoined my bed, an old ewe, the gold smoked herrings slotted behind the rafters, and the little hens under the table; and knew there an intensely happy, intimate peace that was sheer heaven to a child.

From the Mountains we moved to the Midlands, where I first met (and greatly feared) the huge red cows, so different from our small black bullocks. Hereabouts (near Melton Mowbray) I learnt to milk a cow, set a hen, and the farmers' wives taught me to cure bacon and ham, and raise pork pie; and (from the Nottingham side) I learnt of home-made wines, and all the luscious farmhouse cookery. Meanwhile I'd been much down West, where they taught me to make butter by hand and the ways of clotted cream and splits and laver. During the reluctant years that I worked in London I refuged in the Home Counties, and since then have lived in North Wales. (This is an entirely different country, in some ways akin to Northern Ireland, even as South Wales is akin to Southern Ireland, and parts of Southern Ireland to the Devon of Drake and Raleigh.)

This itinerary is an explanation and an apology, that you may condone with me if I have wandered too long in the parts I love best.

The country background has varied, but always, all my life, I have known the kindness of the country people as the one enduring thing of England. My earliest recollection is being carried high on a broad rough shoulder over green grass, and lifted gently down to pick white mushrooms, all wet with rain; of a rag rug and kitchen fender, and the fat cat in my old nurse's cottage; of a people who were never nervy or cross, nor too hurried for a child. Some might be taciturn; but what child minds the friendly silence that lets it chatter away freely, if it can extract a satisfactory grunt at intervals? The country people can give a child the simple necessary kindness and warmth it needs; and for long periods "let you alone" (which is *not* neglect—far otherwise!).

Incidentally, it distresses me when urban-minded novelists

make country people behave passionately like debased idiots. Actually a kindly brought-up country child slides so unconsciously into full knowledge of animal life that her instincts of natural selection are probably as clearly developed as those of any other healthy young animal; and for the lads, if the principles of good breeding are not learnt in the care taken of the male stock of the farmyard (yes, and in the gentle treatment necessary for the breeding animals), I don't know where else they could be better taught. Probably country love-making is more deeply passionate because of this longer unconscious growth in knowledge. In the country child, natural physical development leads to the conscious sorting of unconsciously accumulated facts, and all questions, as a rule, get bluntly truthful but not unkindly answers. It seems to me, in contrast, that the social and mental activity of towns acts as a forcing house of the mind over the immature body; but all this is very controversial, and I put forward these points very humbly.

Educationally, for years the country was at a disadvantage; nowadays better communication and the transfer of older pupils to central schools should make a better type of education available to more children, and give a better chance for the eccentric child to find congenial spirits. But, in vocational training, the opportunities the country child gets to specialise contrast badly with those of the town child, who, for a few shillings a term, can study at excellent evening classes, and find like-minded friends and, more probably, a congenial mate.

Nowadays, in spite of depression, England is a manufacturing country and its people have become largely town dwellers, so that the public outlook and legislation are apt to consider the urban population most readily; but the root of our race is in the healthy happy country life of the island, and it seems to us country folk that we should need less help than the town dwellers, were that help given with as much understanding.

If in these pages I have stressed the pleasant side of our country landscape, it is perhaps because I feel the other side too strongly and personally to be able to write about it. As a child I often visited a gentle old couple in the village, who had lived all their lives together in a small cottage in a garden. In that garden early peas sprouted in spring, and swallows built so low under the eaves that you could peer into the nests. They had a lilac bush by the gate, and a cat who followed them about like a dog and did wonderful tricks.

One day all vanished. I was too young to know why, but later heard the story. They were childless, poor and old, could barely read or write, and grew ill. Helpless, nervous and clinging to each other, they had been driven down to the "House" with their small possessions packed carefully in the back of the cart, and the old cat in a basket at their feet.

At the Workhouse their few goods were confiscated, the old cat promptly drowned, they were each put separately into dormitories full of strangers, and realised that they would never again see each other, except for one hour a day in a public room. Man having usurped Death's cruelty, Death was kind to them, and they died within an hour of each other: died in dumb blank misery and bewilderment as to what wrong they had done to be so punished?

This was years ago, yet the ghost of that tragedy has laid a shadow over the meadows for me ever since. Please believe, if I have not spoken of the sad things of the country, it is because I too am a countrywoman and share them.

The English country people are experienced, resourceful, ingenious, usually excellent craftsmen, with thoughtful careful pride in the goodness of their work. But the countryman is not naturally aggressive or assertive; and he is usually utterly uncommercial. Yet, because the work of countless generations of country people has made this land of England what it is, and is making other great lands abroad, it is surely for Englishmen generally to understand them better, to protect their interests, and to accord to country work the place it deserves in our national life?

The English country has not changed in spirit, and all Englishmen are countrymen at heart; so, if because of these notes some of you may go more directly to the parts of England where you will be happiest, and find the welcome nearest to your liking, that will be the justification of this simple book.

4 SHEEP ON THE ROAD IN THE SOUTH DOWNS

5 THE VILLAGE SHOP

6 LLYN IDWAL, at the foot of Glyder-fawr, Snowdonia

CHAPTER II

MOUNTAIN AND MOORLAND

"The air is piercing, and of a sharp temperature, and would be more biting but for the high hills, which break off the northern storms and cold falling snow. Notwithstanding, rich is this province, and with great varieties of commodities is replenished; the lofty hills, though rough, yet smile upon their beholders, spread with sheep and cattle; the valleys stored with grass and corn sufficient; the sea affordeth great store of fish, and the land is overspread with great variety of fowles."

> MICHAEL DRAYTON, author of *Polyolbion*,
> writing of the Lake District in the early
> seventeenth century.

IT is difficult to write of British mountains when living on one, and our small village is crouched like a rock rabbit on the sloping edge of a mountain . . . it's like criticising one's own grandfather.

The wall stones of our house are cut from the quarry behind, the slates overhead are from Glyndyfrdwy old quarries (where the great forty-feet water wheel now stands moss grown and idle). The little wall that holds us from slipping off the mountain into the river is built of water-worn fossil rocks, from the bed that gurgles past Ty-issa.

Half the larder floor *is* rock, living rock still in the mountain, and they have had to shape the side wall to fit over it. No, the mountain, to one that lives on *the* mountain, is a part of himself, inseparable from his existence. Though you may be bed-ridden indoors, and never set foot outside for weeks, you feel the mountain there, reminding you of its presence day and night. The whiff of peat, wavering from the hearth, drifts like smoke through the senses, all day long, and suddenly there comes the howl and cry of the wind, tearing down from the heights to fling itself against your door, or to lift and lie down with a shudder under your carpet. The queer distinct smell that comes down in the wet weather . . . the sense of a larger presence, always above you, even when thick mist and fog settle down close, and you see no farther than the gate for weeks, make you *feel* the mountain there, always.

I do not know when I would send a visitor on to the mountains. Certainly the hills are lovely in the spring, when April showers have filled the little narrow dales with the crisp foam of whitethorn and the loose sweet laughter of wild cherry, when the freshlets of spring rain are dashing down, in spun foam and silver, when the bogs gleam vivid sheer emerald in the sunlight, and cloud shadows race across. To be up and away in the cold spring dawn on an English mountain! To splash in icy white water, fresh from the frozen snow on the peaks above, snow from drifts that lie melting on the lower pastures, wet and webbed out into a half-ice thin as silk glass, with the spikes of the new green grasses piercing through. Overnight the frozen ice has run, and varnished the rocks, and hangs in long white icicles (that break with musical notes), and there is the tiny thin brittle ice, that rifts out through the small waterfalls, so that they pipe like silver flutes of spring.

In the cold spring days the small fields in the valleys are full of ewes, clustering round strewn hay, and by April white spindle-legged lambs are tottering to shelter against the primrose-covered banks. On the hillside pastures some of the cows are out early, for, in the mountain districts where they make cheese, the best milk of the year comes when the cows still get a mouthful of blown snow with the grass. Though cheese-making belongs to the wider vales, it is claimed by the mountain folk that the "high pastures do feed, and the lower pastures do fill," and the *quality* of the higher pasture cheese is exceptionally good. To these upper pastures the cowherd carries the milking churn strapped on to his back, and a sledge drags the milk churns over the rough mountain trackways down to the valley below.

Then, summer holidays on the mountains! Full summer! When the August heather burns purple, rich and warm, and bees drone, and the sun is molten brass, pouring heat from a brazen sky, and the movement of your knees among the dry, cracking heather stems sends out a peppery cloud . . . when the sheep lie panting under the hot rocks, and a great hawk is painted motionless against the sky. The wide, shelterless moors seethe with heat as no other earth can. Still noonday, not a breath stirring, to lie on your back, cushioned on the springy heather, a few dried stems, rainbow-rimmed, meeting over your face, and the dry metallic curl of bracken, bronzing in the heat, clicking like dry-legged beetles walking.

Every colour of purple, from the northern bluebell heather to the scarlet red ling of the west, grows across our mountains, but how can one give, in one colour word, the burnt rainbow glory of heather, rippling under a moorland wind in wet autumn? When the dry arid smell of the heath-burning hangs in the air, and a long red fire-line wavers across the moors in the dusk. . . .

7 SUMMER OVER TYN-Y-BWLCH, MERIONETH : A small cultivated patch among the Aran Hills

8 WINTER OVER THE YORKSHIRE WOLDS

In autumn come the long dreary days and black nights of rain, when the shepherds must be out constantly, for soon the sheep will be brought down from the hills, the wet hills, where the rowans are scarlet against the witches, and the curlew cries out of the mist, and the ghosts walk through the rushes.

But if I would have strangers know the grandeur of our mountains, and learn fear, then I would send them up the mountains in winter, and the snow, when the precipices are black rifts of rock, and the great winds have swept up their white beds to sleep against the peaks. Then, overhead the moors lie silent, still and white under a grey sky, only the beck shrill-piping its frost song; one single clear sweet note,

MOUNTAIN SLEDGE FOR MILK CHURNS

all night long, telling the mountain village that it is winter —winter on the hills.

To each mountain in England belongs its individuality, and, as with a person, you can say that they *are* so and so, or *do* so and so (but you cannot say whether someone else will like them or not). So with the mountains, they will like you or not, according to your individuality and theirs. The Lake hills of sheep walks and sudden mists, of winding waterfall valleys and peaceful, friendly stone-built villages, and small towns, are perhaps the best known English mountains.

From High Street, where the Roman road leads up to the mountain-top above Mardale, can be seen one of the most wonderful views in all the Lake District. In summer the peaks around gather colour like a giant's garden; in winter they are like a cross-currented sea, white tipped.

The Pennines have a different character, wild and open in the North, but in the Dales district they are perhaps the most

individual of all the hills of England. The Dales of the West
Riding are long parallel green valleys, lying between high spurs
of limestone. Sheep are on the hills, and in the wider valleys
(such as Wensleydale) there are cattle and corn. The higher
Pennines, and certain peaty districts, are bracken- and heather-
clad, but the typical Yorkshire dale lies between grey grass-
crowned hills—a wide, bleak country of grass and rush-green
moorlands, in which the dale is sunk, suddenly, to a narrow
green floor of vivid soft grass, posied with tiny coloured
flowers. Down the middle of the dale, between banks of
gleaming white limestone, runs a trout-beck, clear as crystal
and brown as the spots on its own silver fish.

On the east the Yorkshire moors are very different in
character, brighter in colour and more heather-clad; between
Pickering and Stokesley you may walk over some of the
wildest country in England. It was near Whitby that Cædmon
was born; he was a herdsman, working in St. Hilda's monastery,
and Bede reports that when, after dinner, he saw the harp of
good fellowship approaching, he would get up and move
away lest he should be asked to sing, for he was regretfully
unmusical. . . . And one such night he had gone out as usual to
sleep with his cattle when there woke him a voice telling him
to sing. He replied, "I cannot sing, I have come out here
because I could not sing." But the voice commanded, "Nevertheless, you must sing for me, Cædmon." So Cædmon stood
up in the dark among the rustling straw, and sang for God, and
next day the matter was investigated at the monastery, and
(after due precautions had been taken by the religious authorities to prove that Cædmon's gift was from God and not from
the Devil), the monks read to him portions of the Scriptures,
which he, the herdsman, "gathering into his quiet mind, even
as he gathered his flocks into their fold" by nightfall, turned
into the first poetry of his own people.

The Peak District is absolutely different. Smooth, rounded
hills, or, as on Froggart Edge just outside Sheffield or among
the Peak Caverns, sudden precipitous rocks and steep valleys.
Kinderscout is one of the wildest, and can be one of the wettest,
mountains in England. Glossop Hill stands up over the Black
Country, and then drops steeply down to the yellow-stoned
doorsteps and blackened houses of industrial England. The
Peak Forest, Dove Dale and the wild moorlands lie between
the Potteries and Sheffield. Almost unbelievably isolated are
some of these small inaccessible villages of the Peak. Flash was
snowed up a year ago, and even the questing aeroplanes could
not locate her under the mist and snow, while a few miles

farther on, at Buxton, the cars were swinging by over the cleared high roads.

The Welsh Hills centre around Snowdon in the North and the Beacons in the South. Snowdon has a railway, you may trot up the whole family, including infants in arms, and eat buns and drink tea on the top and spend the night, and see the sunrise, if it doesn't mist. (They can't regulate Snowdon for you, only you for Snowdon.) There's a new hostel at the foot, five different tracks up, and a weighing machine on top, and yet—Snowdon remains dignified Snowdon. Last year I was there when Tryfan was as thick with climbers as flies on a sugar bowl; rock climbers with ropes were learning their holds, walkers were scrambling and slithering down, the place was thick with visitors. It was the first time I had ever seen my grim old Snowdon in the throes of an August summer holiday, and Snowdon looked very happy, as if he were giving a children's party!

The Arenigs are wet, bilberry-covered hills, with the strangest smell of any range in North Wales. Across the tops, direct from Llanwchllyn above Blaenau Festiniog to Moel Siabod, or South to Cader Idris, lie fine ranges, wild wet bog patches, where the will-o'-the-wisp will bounce before you. Ffordd cam Elin (the old route of the Princess) goes back across the Berwyns. Moel Sych guards a little round haunted pool of lily leaves, and St. Dogfan's Well is by Tyn-y-pystll (the waterfall above Llanrhaidr-yn-Mochnant). They say that in one of the valleys below you must not shoot a hare, for there once fled a princess to hide her beauty from love, and pray for holiness, and there came a lord hunting, and his hounds ran the hare close, so that it doubled suddenly and fled, and hid under the edge of the lady's cloak—where she knelt praying. Then the hounds drew off, and the huntsman waited silently, till she arose, her prayers finished, and the hare limped off, unharmed and white as snow. . . .

You must be sure to have some of the home-cured bacon and ham that they make in that valley, and some of the bread that they still bake in their brick ovens, for it is very good.

The Wrekin, in Shropshire, has been sung in *The Shropshire Lad*, and the Breidden are two gracious pointed breasts. On the Malvern Hills, on a May morning, the apple-blossom is pink and sweet above St. Anne's Well. Here *Piers Plowman* was written, and the spring still flows clear and cool—high up above the old abbey.

Go inland, beyond Clun, and onwards over its Forests

(which are really huge bare hills, though you get some new fir-clad slopes); and God! how the wind howls over them!

One night, driving up from the South, the snow caught us where we braved the Border mountains above Newcastle beyond Clun at midnight; so, blinded with the spinning whiteness, we drew in off the lost roadway and built a fire under the dark fir-trees on the sloping hillside and sat watching the firelit scarlet feathers of the snow swirl down, and fall wet and hissing into the crackling pine boughs. . . . Four hours later, emerging into a still white world, we dug out the white round mound that had once been a little car, and broke the white trail, foot by foot, bumping on and off the heathery edge and perilous dykes, down to Newtown and on to Welshpool and Oswestry at daybreak. (Here a constable finding us asleep in the middle of the High Street, tempered justice with mercy and got us drinks through a back door before taking our names and addresses for parking at the front!)

The Beacon Hills farther South are grass and rush covered, and all that land is a land apart. The Farmers of the Beacons are a race apart; to be Shepherd of the Beacons is to be a shepherd of strength, skill, and almost superhuman endurance, for on those grass and reed-covered hills they have some of the worst weather in England. On the Beacons you can be squelching knee-deep in rushes and water and snowdrift in the turn of the wind.

South, into Devon, are the red and brown moors, gold-girt with gorse and rifted red earth. Dartmoor, of the wild ponies and quaking bogs, has a long open road over it, swung like a whip lash between the rocky tors. This moorland is small in acreage, but wide as the wind, and mysterious with sweeping grey mists. Here are circles of grey stone, great cromlechs, and small stone cottages, and villages that climb up into the heart of the moor. Princetown prison is there, grim and grey. On Dartmoor there are tiny lost forests, barely six foot high, but bent and twisted among the rocks, incredibly full of small live things and old dead magics. Here are trout streams, and the smell of peat smoking in the evening dusk.

Off Dartmoor you drop through steep hollow lanes deep down into warm Devon valleys full of sunshine, daffodils, honeysuckle and roses, with cob cottages, roofed with piebald, golden-patched thatches. Along the coast are little warm inlets of the sea, steep-sided, that catch the sun and are full of the scent of gorse, and there are patches of golden sands and the small bathing coves among the stern cliffs are unexpected and happy as chuckles in a grim story.

9　MOEL SIABOD, at 2,865 feet in the Carnarvonshire Hills.
There is fine fishing in the lake

10　HORNED SHEEP ON SHARP TOR, DARTMOOR

Exmoor, of the haunted derelict mining-shafts, is, perhaps, harder in character and has even deeper sea mists. Here, in places, great cliffs break from the moor top straight down to the foam of the sea. In the land behind there lived the old stern race of the miners, who put sheep's blood in their cider and made their own grim laws, and the dark brown "wreckers-men" and smugglers who evilly infested the sea. An old trick of theirs was to fasten a stable lantern to the horns of a cow and set her wandering along the cliff edge in the dark, so that the light swaying like a ship at sea should mislead the mariners, and their wrecked cargo strew the rocks below. . . . But one dark night they caught a Spaniard, rich prize; and on board there was a priest of Power, and he cursed them as he drowned, and that curse holds to-day. . . .

Hereabouts, in stone cottages between the cliffs, are twisted stairways, and in damp weather the driftwood treads and ship-timbered beams smell of cherrywood and spice, ghost spirits from the brandy casks that burst under them. But all the fine bales of Brussels net are worn out, thin as mist and perished away; only the torn shreds trail over the gorse bushes in the wet. Sea-damp lace, over gold, above the smugglers' cove. . . .

MOUNTAIN INDUSTRIES

"O, the bonny woo'ly sheep,
  Feedin' on the mountain steep,
  Bleat ye! bleat ye! as ye go!
  Thro' the winter frost and sno',
  Hart, nor hind, nor fallow deer,
  No by half, so useful are
  Fra' king to lads that hauds the plough
  All gi' praise to tarry woo'."

Old Spinning Song

Sheep are the main industry of the hill farms, and the breeds of the sheep in most cases are closely connected with the hills and of types adapted to them, though several breeds, notably the Cheviots, spread on to other mountains, and some old breeds tend to die out. For example, the old Yorkshire lank has disappeared, but the small Welsh sheep is localised, and so are the Herdwicks of the Lakes (there is no animal more compact and trim and agile than a stout little Herdwick hog). Moorland sheep differ entirely from the fat, stupid sheep of the Shires, or the plump, peaceable sheep of the Downs. They have slight connection with some marsh sheep (such as those of

Romney Marsh), but sheep-walking on the mountains is a completely different thing from sheep fattening in the Shires. The breeding times are different, and so is the whole management of the flock. What time the South lambs are fat and ready for mint sauce, the hill ewes are lambing in the lowland pastures.

The hill shepherd is a lean man, of great endurance and wide knowledge of mountains and flocks—he is out in all weathers over the hilltops with his dogs. As a rule he substitutes a stout stick for the crook (except when the flocks are down in the folds). Frequently he wears his old plaid, especially in the spring, the two long loops hung over the shoulder on either side making convenient slings for a pair of lambs dropped on the mountain, and so he carries them down, the old ewe trotting behind. He frequently follows the medieval custom of taking with him "his tar box and his scrip," that is the tar foot dressing, to be applied after paring a hoof or cleaning a scar, and his own personal provision of food and drink, in case he is caught out overnight and must needs take shelter in one of the top huts.

The mountain sheep do not have bells and are more wild than docile, yet in spite of months of absence on the moors, many of the sheep (especially the ewes, who have been nursed down in the home paddocks), still know their shepherd as well as the Southdown sheep know theirs; and though on the whole the mountain flocks scatter widely, yet you will often find a shepherd miles away on the moors, with some old ewe sturdily following him, friendly, and crowding up for bits of bread out of the lunch bag.

Usage varies according to the mountain. Roughly, the sheep go up on to the hills to the early spring grass "as soon as there is a good bite," and sometimes before or after that date the ewes and lambs join them. The entire flock stays on the hills till late autumn; the sheep do not move about haphazard; apart from the jurisdiction of the shepherd and the grazing rights, the wise old leaders of the flock work out a pretty adequate forage system for themselves. The black-faced sheep were notoriously good foragers! Mountain sheep *do think*; those narrow tracks among the heather are beaten out by generations of tiny hooves trotting steadily from one definite spot to another. Good scratching stumps, or dry nooks under overhanging rocks, are hunted up, and peat ledges, sheltered and warm, are regularly sheep-claimed dormitories. If you happen to be caught out by mist, and spend the night in one, presently will come trotting feet, and the worried woolly face

11 BREAKFAST IN THE SNOW

12 SMALL LAMBS AND BIG TURNIPS

13 WENSLEYDALE IN THE PENNINES : Famous for Cheese-grazing

14 THE CHEVIOT HILLS AND THE OLD LINE OF THE ROMAN WALL

of the owner will peer at you reproachfully, and bleat and hang about for hours, waiting impatiently for you to get up and let her come to her bed (or, if it's the old ram and his favourites, I wouldn't put it past him getting the better of the argument!). These details of sheep mentality are proven by those who know the hills intimately. An old shepherd and myself spent one summer mapping the moorland, as his sheep had "worked it out for themselves." It was a curious piece of work, and very enlightening as to the mentality of mutton. Direct routes led to the watercourses and best grazing ground—devious ways crossed several dangerous bogs, and there were short cuts through unprofitable heather patches. Stunted hill trees, cool rocks shady for noonday heat, etc., were well mapped out. Memory was shown around the old salting places, and enterprise leading to the new. Some specially cropped patches the shepherd believed were the result of their partiality for certain herbs (some wild thyme, and the brown tassels of the rushes were well nibbled). Other places too were obviously popular, but for some sheep reason we could not discover. But quite reasonably by the time of the day, the time of the season, by position on the hills and turn of the weather, *do the sheep order themselves about*, and a flock having leaders that know the mountains will get better feeding from it, and make itself more comfortable than newcomers.

Hill rams are fine fighters; they face one another, breathing heavily, and stamp about for some time before battle—then go at it full tilt, head on, bang! Their curling horns and hard skulls meet with a steady hammer blow that can be heard for miles. Then they turn, trot back solemnly, face one another again—and await the other's readiness before charging full tilt for another head-on crash.

They say that the Crusaders brought back tilting from the fighting rams of the east. If jousts were half as exciting as a hill-ram fight I don't wonder they were so popular. The rams of some of the old, very pugnacious mountain breeds used to be fitted with leather caps through the summer to prevent the flies laying their eggs where they abrased themselves in the fighting. The first and best prize at mountain shows is for *"One ram and three sheep straight from the mountain,"* because that class shows really good shepherding.

Because the mountain sheep (especially the larger Northern breeds) are naturally defensive, the shepherd dog in the North is sometimes trained to throw the ram before he can drive down the sheep. This is done either by a skilful thrust at the shoulder, or by hanging on to the rump, and dodging as the

D

ram turns. Once the ram is out of the way the dog can drive
the flock where he will. A clever dog can sometimes raise
thrown sheep (for sheep if they fall awkwardly cannot get
up). This is a difficult feat, but unfortunately any training which
allows the dog to touch the sheep prevents that dog from
competing in the sheep-dog trials of Southern districts, where,
with the small lighter sheep, it disqualifies him if he so much
as touches one.

The technique for shepherd and dog when herding strong
agile hill flocks and covering great distances is very different
from the technique of shepherd and dog working with the
lowland, or down, sheep. The collie is still in use in the North,
and sometimes a reprehensible mongrel strain will develop a
good sheep-dog; but the majority of better dogs are the result

of years of breeding, and the comparatively small long-haired black
collie breed, with a white tip to
its tail, is the typical sheep-dog.
It would be interesting to investi-
gate if some of the call notes in
use (especially in some Welsh
mountains) have any connection
with the old Cistercian music
notes which were, I believe, based
on chants. One Welsh shepherd I
knew years ago had the name of
"Dirandie" (the blackbird) because

ON WATCH

of his whistling notes to his dog. All shepherds have their own
ways of training dogs—generally speaking, for a mountain sheep-
dog we have, variously, "*Way Out*" (on a rising inflection):
that is, "farther away in the direction you are going"; "*Come
in*" (two notes dropping): that is "in towards the shepherd";
"*G'behind*," "*Heel*"; "*Down*": that is "drop flat on the earth and
remain motionless"; "*Sound*," "*Speak*," or "*Bark*" (this last seldom used at close quarters, though an experienced dog working
far out on the hills will sometimes use it on his own initiative,
to rouse sheep that he sees at a distance, above or below him).
"*Over*" signifies to "get over the dyke," or the ditch; "*Ware,
ware*," or "*Seek, seek, seek*," is to scout around in a wide circle,
to clear a field, or round up stragglers. "*Kep*," "*Bide*," or
"*Watch*," means "keep an eye on them sheep and don't let
them move from there, while I go and get a drink" (or
whatever else the shepherd wants it to mean!), but this
vocabulary must necessarily be very general, and I give
only the words I have actually known in use.

15 LATE SNOW IN THE CHEVIOTS

16 BRINGING DOWN THE FLOCKS FOR SHEARING
FROM THE COTSWOLD HILLS

For show purposes in sheep-dog trials the dogs may be trained to almost automatic exactitude and obedience and only two or three notes, but the perfect understanding between some shepherds and their dogs seems to require no words at all. Some of the most useful, experienced hill dogs make a poor display in the show field; I've recollections of one dog of extraordinary sagacity whose master tried him out according to "show" methods. Three times that dog penned the same sheep faultlessly, and then, when for the third time we deliberately released those sheep for no cause, he rushed anxiously back to the shepherd, and sitting down before him peered up into his face with such an expression of horrified enquiry that the proceedings abruptly broke up!

The season when young lambs and ewes rejoin the flock after the washing and shearing takes place depends on district and climate. In the hills, if possible, the sheep are kept down after the washing till after the dipping, branding and earmarking of the youngsters; and everything is done in one job. A sheep-washing, or dipping day, resounds half down the valley; in the mountains a convenient stream is blocked up, convenient pens built, and though the actual washing may only take one complete day's hard work, a careful medical dipping, and cleaning up may last an entire week. Though dipping and washing are different processes, the proceeding is pretty much the same to watch. There are the pens of waiting sheep, with dogs on guard, four or five men standing by the dip; the draining pen; the shepherd (with his footknife and dopes of dressing and boxes of various bug salves); the detention pen for "cases"; and the two working sheep-dogs ready to chase a runaway. Sheep must dry in clean pasture; the yolk (that is the natural fat) must be worked back into the wool, and the wool must have sufficient time to interlock its strands again and "fleece" before shearing. Shearing is sometimes done by hand, and sometimes by machinery.

In mountain districts it is still customary to hold large sheep-shearing parties in turn at each farm. Usually a barn is cleared, or some sort of shelter put up, straw stacks are thrown down on a clean rick cloth, and there's a regular set-to with beef sand-wiches, fresh mustard, cheese, beer, jokes, the news of the district and some courting. The fleeces are taken off differently according to the district; sheep are queerly patient of this operation, though a young one may raise a kick or two, or break away, tearing the fleece. But mostly they lie quiet enough in good hands. One worker stands aside and rolls up the fleece instantly, white shining side outwards; the loose pieces are packed into the middle, the neck wool is pulled out into a long twisted rope, which the fleece packer binds round and tucks in to form a handle, and then the fleeces are stored in a dark barn till sold. They "give" a little, and stir for some time, being yet live wool. There is nothing so white and soft as a new warm fleece roll, unless it be a head of thistledown in the sun. In the barn, where the dusty light spears down in level shafts through the shutter chinks, the white fleece gleams like a moonstone. Close clipping shows up any sores or scars on the sheep, besides any accidental jabs in clipping, though this accident is uncommon, for old hands will clip for years and never "break wool." The shepherd is in attendance on every sheep, clearing up the scrotum, feeling the ewes' udders, examining ears, eyes and mouth, dressing hooves, etc. Incidentally, an old teapot with the spout hammered out makes a very handy pot for sheep dressing and pours down the cracks of the parted wool very neatly! I've found one or two well-abused old pewter and tin coffee-pots left behind in derelict shepherd huts on the mountains.

When the last sheep is passed as "fit for the mountain," and the fleeces are rolled, the chaps throw in their caps and it is hey! for the hills—as soon as the sheep are marked.

Sheep are marked variously; in the mountains buisting with tar is usual, the owner's letter, or the grazing mark, shaped in iron, is dipped into hot tar and pressed quickly against the sheep's side, and the mark lasts pretty clear till the next shearing.

The earmarks of sheep are so specific that they are still the countryman's name for breeding. As the country people put it, "he should be a likely lad, his earmarks are good on both sides of the family." These ear notches are still used, especially for pedigree flocks, or where a change in type is being tested, though the more complicated earmarkings are less favoured nowadays. The female has one notch, or small hole punched in the near ear, the male lamb in the far ear. (This is after castration.) Twin ewes have a hole in each ear; a special ewe, to be watched as a breeder of future tups, may have two holes in the near ear (hence the point of earmarks, to show select breeding); or the shepherd will hall-mark a special line in breed by a small triangle of three holes punched close together (and perhaps the rest of the flock will go unmarked).

It is a cause of wonder to the uninitiated how a shepherd can distinguish as individuals such a number of animals so superficially alike as sheep. In *The Times* a judge expressed astonishment that a shepherd claimed to know "about sixty" sheep "by their faces," and yet that number is far exceeded by many shepherds, who will not only know the sheep individually, but in the case of ewes will give you years, dates, numbers of lambs, etc., for three generations.

Sheep are brought down off the hills in the autumn, and the sheep drives over the Berwyns, or the clearing of Snowdon, or the Beacon, are great moorland fêtes. The owners of the grazing, shepherds' dogs and drivers, sweep over the hillside in a wide curve. The best place to watch is from the gathering point below. There may be some shouting and riding, and sounds afar of the work going on overhead, but in the meeting place among the foothills all will be quiet. . . . There will be bird-calls, streams singing quietly through the bronzing heather, and you and the waiting shepherds may drowse for hours before the circle closes in. . . . Then, presently, down the gulleys above, there begins to pour a grey trickle of sheep; they come slowly, but gradually, and while you watch, another gully fills, till presently the whole hillside is covered with a gently moving mantle of live grey wool, centralising to the meeting place. Quick scampers of outsiders, half a dozen sheep or so, with the sheep-dog rounding them in, keep joining the main mass, all moving downwards, till presently the smooth grey stream of trotting sheep is a pool spread out in the valley, and the sheep-dogs rush round, turning the wanderers inwards, till there is a compact, smooth pool of grey. Then the sheep-dogs gather to their masters, white tail tips swaying, tongues hanging out, laughter shaking from their ears and shining in their quick watchful eyes. It is the one day above all others of the year that the sheep-dog enjoys most thoroughly ! Gradually the collected sheep are worked out down the pass into the level and the sorting pens. If they pass along a high road, two dogs only go weaving backwards and forwards behind them, keeping the flock gently on the move, while the other dogs wait ready on either side, instantly quick to head off any attempt to leave the road or break away from the main current. Some shepherds ride on ahead and warn cars from the road, for so densely does a big sheep drive fill the valley that any traveller caught before it may well have to wait over an hour before the flock has passed.

The night the sheep are "down" is the first night of winter, and the mountain is left lonely, lonely as the single lost lamb who wanders frantically among the rocks, searching for his vanished company and crying out through the mist for the end of the world.

SHEEP PRODUCTS

Very hard white mutton suet is the basis of some reading-lamp candles, Stearic candles, much harder than the usual tallow mixtures. These are used, of necessity, in all candle lanterns, where the softer wax would melt; also for night lights and religious ceremonies. The sheep's intestines are used for cords for tennis racquets, and guts of that sort; in the old days they were used for harp strings. Actually, some old shepherds (or some very particular ones) still prefer to make their own lanoline for the ewes' udders at lambing time, and in the hills the mutton fat, or mutton marrow, takes the place of the goose grease used by the valley and lowland people as kitchen medicine, for ointment and salve. When melting down the extra fat in the farmhouse, the scraps left at the bottom of the iron pan are called "scratchings" (similarly in rendering pork fat), and are made into a rich meaty pastry, considered a delicacy while fresh. If there are too many, the sheep-dog gets them.

Mutton hams are made in many mountain districts and so are mutton sausages—in fact, the higher up the mountains you go, the more the sheep takes the place of the pig.

Where the moorlands sweep down to the seacoast and the fisher communities have taught the hill people the use of anti-scorbutics, mutton fat, rather than lard, is especially used as a basis for a "green salve" which combines the curative properties of broom buds, water-cress juice, etc., with the emollient nature of the fat. Otherwise, the gathering of the yellow broom to make a lotion for scab cure went entirely out with the use of tar and tobacco juice. The old saying, "It's a pity to spoil a good ship for a ha'porth of tar" refers probably to a "sheep" not a "ship."

Sheeps' horns nowadays go to the bone dust mills, though a few of the finest Highland ones, banded with silver and amethyst, and inset with cairngorm, are sold at Inverness to foreign visitors.

WOOL

As a natural corollary to the sheep on the hillside, a small wool mill is to be found on nearly every stream in the mountain valleys. Nothing shows the centralising of industry and increase of communication more than the disuse of these small wool mills. Apart from the economic and labour side (which had its worst aspect in the child labour of the North), the reason for the local disuse of many of these mills is difficult to follow.

17　MILLDALE, OFF DOVEDALE, DERBYSHIRE.
The stone-dyked road threads the hills

19 LIME-BURNING IN KENT

18 AN OPEN QUARRY-WORKING

Local dyestuffs usually supply the sober ground colouring, supplemented by bought dyes to brighten things up (sometimes disastrously from the aesthetic point of view). Both in the North and West several old mills are now specialising on traditional work. For example, some of the old square designs of the Carnarvonshire blankets are thoroughly satisfying, especially so when worked out in natural black and brown coloured wools, interspersed with the cream and grey of the local breeds, somewhat as in the original Shetland Island work.

Local demand for thick fisherman's stockings, plough breeches, or special jerseys or mits for different outdoor work, have often kept alive home spinning and knitting industries in certain districts, more especially perhaps where the rather long-haired wool, undressed and very rain-resisting, makes the home product more satisfactory in wear than any softer substitute.

In some districts, near fishing lakes or the sea, where there is a market to summer visitors, tweeds, shawls and local made, rather "arty" products have a ready sale in the summer, and cover expenses; in the winter months these mills carry on with their own local products, or do odd jobs for the neighbourhood.

MINERALS

Characteristically, England differs from most of Europe in her division of mines and quarries. In most languages the division is made according to the mineral, or substance, which is mined or quarried, and this is constant whether that particular mineral is mined below ground or above it. Contrariwise, we tend to mine below ground and quarry above, so that Bath stone, or slate, may be mined, or quarried, or a quarry may be underground in a mine.

Cornwall, famed since Phoenician days for tin and lead, is battered and heaved up with old shafts and gorse- and heather-overgrown workings. The characteristic Cornish smelting houses stand empty and stark against the sky, but the far-off descendants of the old square Cornish stamping mills thud their pioneer way over half the world.

Gold mining at present is in a very interesting state in England. Wherever the white line of gold-bearing quartz crisps over the Welsh mountains, or dips by the slate, have cropped up a line of small stamping mills; some are old mines reopened, while others are new ventures which the increase in the value of gold has set working. The coal mines proper, and the mining industry, really belong to town life, but it is curious how long the small mine worker and the smaller mining communities

remain rural even after their cottages and small-holdings have
become absorbed in town planning. They are the people of
the allotments, and when the town has finally absorbed them,
they take along with them their pigeons, dogs and fancy
poultry, remaining country people at heart.

Your quarryman is necessarily a countryman. The feeling
for stone is inborn, and only people who have lived in old
quarry districts realise how completely the stone is a part of
the life of the country. The nucleus of two or three small
towns (the exasperated despair of reformers!) have been the
abandoned sites of adjacent worked-out quarry faces. Upon
these the old workers have "squatted" with that unnoticed
persistency, neglected indifference, or friendly tolerance that

COTTAGE HOME OF THE STONE DISTRICTS

produce our maze of involved boundary lines! The changes in
a stone district always show far more alteration than in a
brick, timber, or purely agricultural district. Of old, when the
quarries were working, every man in the district *thought* in
stone—their houses were well built of enduring stone (the one
material that they knew the worth of, and understood). Walls,
dykes, causeways, everything required, was carried out in the
local stone, by local workers, as a matter of course. If a man
wanted a shed in his garden, or a spare sleeping-room or coal-
shed beyond his house, it was not a case of employing builders;
he himself (with his mates) built it as a matter of course,
consulting nobody (least of all an architect or a landlord)
and simply *taking* the stone and putting it where he liked.

It is incredible to an urban-minded and tape-measured community how much of this sort of thing went on. Rock is comparatively simple to move on a down grade. A small amount of
necessary blasting was arranged for, quietly with a friend, and,

20 CWMPARC, a Mining Village in the Rhondda Valley, looking to the Brecon Beacons

21 A FARMHOUSE ON THE EDGE OF DARTMOOR

at the end of ten years or twenty, behold! your grandson sells a "stone holding" and his son lives in a raw-red bungalow. Yes, the transport of brick and the importation of ready-made timber for building purposes have very far-reaching effects in a stone district, as far-reaching as the supply of steel girders for structure has in building a town.

Among stones, slate holds a unique position. Slate quarrying employs whole districts in North Wales, and (though hundreds of small slate quarries are now abandoned) the huge Bethsaida ones are still among the most impressive mountain sights we have. Among old slate workers there are still men who carve and cut the slate with an almost uncanny comprehension of its brittle possibilities. In a slate district, walls are of slate, fences are made of split posts of slate pierced by holes through which wire is strained. Houses and build-ings have slate floors; in some cases the inner wall divisions, both in houses and farm buildings, are slabs of split slate. Cattle troughs and corn bins are built in of fine grooved slabs of slate. In the better houses shaped slabs of it make the fireplaces and stairways, and these, greased and polished (of old, with hot mutton fat), have the dull gleam of frozen ebony. Dairy shelves,

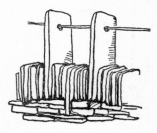

SLATE FENCING

walls and floors made of black slate are the best in the world.

Where some smaller slate quarry is still working on splitting and shaping, you get the most technically interesting and pictorially beautiful industry of the mountains. To realise how very beautiful this black and white can be, go up to the quarry in the spring, when the black wet rocks cut starkly through the late snow on the crags above. Here is sheer-cut intense simplicity of line, as hard and tense as the metallic music of the slate cracking. Cold slate! the white mountain light and freezing rain key it to an icy silver and tense blackness. Then, if it is late spring, and perhaps in a sheltered corner, there bends across the stone (with almost unbearable delicacy and softness) the loose sweet whiteness of a blossoming wild cherry-tree. . . . The icy cold wind, set sharp from the melting snow on the rocks above, shakes the pliant boughs, and a snowdrift of petals floats down against the wet slate—and clings—its frail whiteness turning to the white of ground glass, wet-held against the jet black slate! O! the purity of black and white in a slate quarry in spring, caught below with the

E

small vivid emerald green of the spring grass! Then, by contrast, in the dusty sheds, bronze green of an old work coat and the old ivory yellow and thousand-wrinkled face, and bright blue eyes, of the oldest quarryman, whose brown leather-padded hands knap and split the slate with such incredible dexterity.

And the beauty and blessed living vitality of glowing red fire, and cans of hot strong tea, for a frozen artist petrified by sheer beauty and cold!

Lime quarrying is another mountain industry, though as a rule the quarries occur at a lower level, and the lime kilns burn below them, almost to the valley floor. Again, this industry has become much more centralised. There used to be old lime kilns dotted about all over England, each farm that had any lime material available burning its own, but now the tendency is to have fewer and larger kilns. An interesting point in all quarrying is the use of gravity for transporting the heavy material down the mountain. Sometimes there is a direct sloping way, straight as a streak down the hillside, sometimes the "tram-line" meanders round in wide circles, working out the gradient till the trucks crank and rattle down to the level below. In the small quarries, engine power is used *only* for the rock drills. Incidentally, paper and pencil are fidgety things, and I should think the last tally system in England will be found working in the last stone quarry, for leather-tabbed tallies, and thick-holed wooden boards with counting pegs, are still the easiest use.

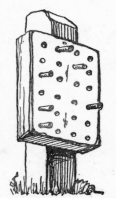

OLD TALLY-BOARD
IN A QUARRY

Because attached to the lime quarries, the smouldering lime kilns, where white smokes trail out of the valleys, may be considered as mountain industries. Some of the foundations for the present kilns are incredibly old, replaced and repaired past counting. The fires are started as a rule with local timber and transported anthracite; once going they will continue for months.

Incidentally, liming land is considered one of the most unpleasant jobs on the farm. An old protection was to smear hands, face and neck with thick cream or butter, and the horse's eyes and nostrils were anointed in the same way. (The other animals used to help him lick off the remains!) Like all country jobs, the pleasantness or otherwise depended a great

22 A STONE HOUSE WEDGED BETWEEN THE CORNISH HILLS,
by Tintagel

23   A LAKELAND HOMESTEAD ABOVE AMBLESIDE

deal on the suitability of the weather; in a shifty wind it was hellish, or impossible.

Cement works, and "road metal" works, are also quarry industries belonging to hilly districts, and in some cases brick and coarse pottery earth are found sufficiently high up on the mountains to make heather packing and gravity transport useful considerations. Much coarse pottery is packed in ling, heather or specially grown rye straw.

The building of the dry stone dykes and sheepstells is extraordinarily skilled craftmanship. No mortar is used, the only tools are a quarryman's "chip" pick and a plumb line. Some of the larger foundation rocks may be anything up to four or five feet square; the subsequent rocks are raised, wedged and fitted above these foundation rocks in regular courses, incredibly interlocked for security, the whole trend of each individual layer sloping downwards and outwards from the centre of the dyke, both for rain shed and stability. The "top-

MOORLAND SHEEPSTELL WITH HAY-RACK INSIDE

ping" of the dyke had to be wedged in, immovably, to the underlying structure, so that it was not easy for mountaineering sheep, or a crossing trespasser, to dislodge the coping, nor, in windswept localities, for drifted snow to weigh down, or melting ice dislodge, the coping stones. It is almost impossible nowadays to find labourers even capable of doing this skilled work, and the cost is economically prohibitive. Many of the round (or crescent-shaped) sheepstells on the moors are of great antiquity, and still used occasionally as an emergency shelter. The old use of them dates from times when arable land in the valley was more valuable, winter feeding less practical, and larger flocks stayed up on the hills further into the winter. Large flocks could be collected into these stells, and maintained safely for a week or so during heavy snow. If you notice, the position and shaping of the stells allow for the prevailing wind (and probably a snow-drift) to form sheltering barriers against the stell. The treading of the sheep themselves within would effectually prevent burying, but care had to be taken against overheating. Some stells show the marks, about three feet from the ground, where timbers were built out from the walls to hold hay supplies, and assist the shepherd and dog to prevent accidents from overcrowding.

PEAT

Peat smoke of the mountains! The magic arid air greets you suddenly, and stirs a subtle unrest in the homesick mountaineer pent in the lowlands. Peat fuel is in general use all over the mountains, and most of the mountain holdings include "peat rights." The cutting has to be adapted to the conditions of the peat. Typically, there are deep, wet peats, and heavy ones;

PEAT-CUTTING

shallow peats, and dry; while surface peat, which is light, and has an industry of its own, is sifted and exported as peat-moss litter, as packing for various trades. Dark heavy peats are slow to dry, slow to burn and give out a steady, intense heat; the lighter peats reduce to ash more quickly (even flame a little sometimes), but the typical peat fire is the slow one, long-enduring.

The majority of peats are cut (after the surface has been pared back) in "faces" of the greatest depth possible according to the peat-face. The turf-cutting spade varies tremendously locally. In many places in the West it is similar to the long-handled Irish turf-cutter, but I have seen turves cut on the old "Devonshiring" method on parts of Dartmoor. The heart-shaped spade is dragged along in a horizontal surface cut, one man pulling before and the other pushing behind, against a cross bar level with the thighs. This is an old method, that was used for removing the surface off the land, for burning the tilth; it is a method often used for cutting burning turf, though similar to the way they cut turves for laying down grass, or topping walls (i.e. dykes), or for cutting turves for thatch-covering or other purposes. Slices of grassy turf are always useful, and so usually, in a district where peat fuel is called "turves," you will find one of these old horizontal cutting spades in the cartshed. A usual "peat" is twelve to eighteen inches long, four to eight inches square, the long narrow spade having one flange turned up to give the slicing cut to the downward shove. You cut downwards in lines, working across the face of the peat, in steps.

SHELTER IN A PEAT-STACK

The bottom of the cut usually soaks full of dark peat-water. The peats dry, laid on the surface of the moor, flat out, or propped up in cloves. Towards autumn, when (perhaps!) dry, they are carried down by mountain pony and sledge, or by cart, or in panniers of rough osier-work across a pony; or I have seen a line of women carrying them in great fan-backed creels, the protective fan rising high above their heads. They were walking in file down the mountain-side, carrying the peats, and knitting as they went (but this was on the Western seaboard).

The peats are stacked convenient to the house; sometimes they are thatched over with reeds or bracken, sometimes they are built up over a few pieces of wood into an open shelter, for hens or the pig, through the winter months. This is a very convenient thing to do, because it's somewhere for the animals to keep dry through the worst of

FIRESIDE PEAT-
BREAKER

the weather, and it lets air into the middle of the stack. When the turves are used up, then winter is over, and the animals don't want the shelter any more. Going into an empty cottage or cabin, you can tell when the owner will be coming back by the way the fire is left. If the woman-of-the-house will have cooking to do on her return, the fire will be strong below but well battened down, with some thick dry peats on top, and wet ones laid flat over all; and there will be spare peats put to dry around, close so that they will be ready to burn quickly when she is ready to open her fire and start cooking. If the shepherd is alone, and not likely to be back until the next day, the peats will *all* be laid close, and flat, round a little fire, and "smothered in" with a thick layer of damp peats, and the waiting drying peat will not be set too close.

MOUNTAIN CORN

The slow peat fire of the mountains cooked the mountain foods to perfection. Porridge cooked over peat is just about perfect. The saying of mountain mutton, "fatter in the valley but sweeter on the hill," holds somewhat for mountain corn. It is seldom one gets enough sun for wheat, but quick sun and hill wind will ripen oats, and Scotch oats are, of course, well known. (I believe it is a fairly established fact that the mountain oats in most districts have special qualities from the soil, if not the weather.) In some districts they still grow special varieties. Oats and barley will both grow where wheat will not; until quite recently bread made from rye and various meslins could be bought at Penrith and in other hill districts. Mutton and oats were the mainstay diet of the mountains. The original brose was just oatmeal put into the shepherd's hoggin and carried dry until an hour or two before needed when he filled the hoggin from some mountain stream, and as he carried it slung over his shoulder, the continuous shaking and churning produced a cold broth, a drink considered more sustaining, because more slowly assimilated, than the heat-cooked porridge. The broth from the slow-stewing mutton was also thickened with oatmeal into a meat porridge, and the oats cooked with marrow made a pudding. Ordinary "porridge," with salt and milk, was part of the regular provender dealt out to visiting harvesters twice daily in all mountain districts. Browis was oat-bread (or oatcake), crumbled into a basin of boiling water, or with hot broth poured over it. The former, with a lump of butter, and pepper and salt, is the "brewis," or tea-kettle broth, of the West,

OLD STYLE SHEPHERD'S HOGGIN

24 CARTING LONG-CUT PEAT ON BODMIN MOOR, CORNWALL

25 BRACKEN AND WOODLAND AT GRINDLEFORD,
near Sheffield

26 A MOORLAND RIVER : The Bovey, on the
East Side of Dartmoor

still in everyday use (I've had pints of it!). And I know that various forms of oatcake are found in each mountain region.

Haggis is, of course, the lights and trimmings of the sheep, minced and melied with oatmeal, seasoned with mountain thyme, spices, etc. I have seen this made by the old method, which boiled the lights in an iron pot, slowly over a peat fire, the windpipe dangling down and dripping on to the hearth. The "pikelets" of Lancashire, and "light cakes" of the Berwyns, are the "crumpets" of the Midlands, but thinner, and browned, with the admixture of mountain corn to the wheat flour. They sell piles in Oswestry market.

BOILING HAGGIS

HEATHER, BRACKEN, ETC.

Heath-burning has statutory dates and rights. The growth of the heather (ling) is such that only the young early shoots are available for grazing fodder. After some years the woody stems raise the heath plant so high that the land becomes useless for sheep-grazing, and unmanageable for traverse of any sort. In small patches among the mountains, where the heath has escaped burning, you will find it waist-high, very woody, and the black peat-ground below practically bare. The ling therefore is burnt down each year in long sweeps of fire, set against the wind. The job may occupy a few people, or may call out an entire countryside. This systematic burning is very different from the devastation of hill burning which follows accidental firing at the wrong season. The accidental fires not only destroy the grazing, but give the poor small animals little chance to escape, and the most pathetic thing is to find the little dump of scorched feathers that was a bird, helplessly burnt to death on a useless nest. At the right time of the year ling is cut for many uses. Near the Potteries, or where coarse earthenware, thick drainpiping, cattle troughs and such-like heavy earthenware is made, the springy ling makes the best packing possible; also it is used for thatching on sheds, shelters and some small stone houses. It is very durable and long-lasting, though somewhat difficult to use on account of its resilience. Brooms and brushes (besom) are made of the ling. Sometimes single workers, sometimes small communities, covenant for the cutting of a suitable patch and the sledging of it to their sheds. A primitive knee-grip vice holds the wooden strands of the ling compactly, while they are bound with wooden "withys" (i.e. splits-up off a soaked ash log), or with strong osiers, or strips of bark, or any binding common to the district. An axe, knife

KNEE-GRIP VICE FOR
BINDING LING

to trim with, and supply of stakes from the underwood for "tails," and there is a very serviceable broom factory for local use, though it cannot compete nowadays with the cheap imported stuff.

Bracken is cut as part of the regular hill-farm harvest. (Bracken is a sure soil indicator that betrays intractable peat.) It stacks very compactly, and cuts into bales remarkably close and well. It is a very good dry litter for stable and cowshed, and is considered the best footing for corn-stacks, especially if used to a good depth, as it is believed that rats will not penetrate it (though this is non-proven). It is also a non-conducting warm bedding for animals. For this reason also it is used among the hills (as also in East Anglia) for stacking root crops; clamps of potatoes in bracken keep remarkably clean and sound. It is usually brought down on sledges.

Sphagnum moss gathering is a very small industry of the mountains, which developed during the Great War, chiefly owing (I believe) to the inspiration of a town chemist who realised the value of the purity, and intensely absorbent properties, of this material. It smells strongly of iodine and will absorb many times its own weight in water, so that it makes one of the finest possible dressings for suppurating or draining cases. It is a natural deodorant, and can be sterilised and compressed for convenience in use and lightness of transport. The delicious green, feathery moss growing on the hillside, or

27   STAINTHORPE: A Typical Stone Hamlet in Ribblesdale, On the Pennine Divide

28 MALHAM, YORKSHIRE: The Stone-dyked Road and Fell-side

dripping from the pony's panniers as he scrambles down the mountain, may be met again in the white aseptic wards of London's hospitals.

Bilberries, variously called "whortleberries," "worts," "blae-berries," "whinberries," "hurts," or "hurtleberries" (in the South) are a regular Norseman's foot of a plant, being found in Norway and Sweden. Bottles of the juice "as supplied to the King of Norway" are imported by town stores, but up in the mountains we supply ourselves—the berries are very plentiful in certain districts. Sometimes parties from a village will go out by the day, women and children together, with tin cans, gathering the bilberries, and one of the menfolk will promise to meet them and drive them back, when it grows too dark to see the small purple berries among the green. Or the gipsies will bring down bilberries, gathering them from where they camp on the mountain-side and selling the luscious purple fruit in dripping scoopfuls at the back doors. On some hills we get wild raspberries, but the best blackberries are not on the hills, but in the narrow sheltered hill valleys, where they hang down over the water, or sweep across the stone-footed dykes, and these blackberries have a richness unknown in the Mid-lands. The blackberries are so thick and plentiful in some mountain districts that lorries come down, with dealers, who buy them up, at prearranged hill depots, as well as the usual country markets. Ripe blackberries are sometimes a full inch across, and large as garden loganberries, and simply full of juice, probably on account of the wet land, or from the small water-courses near which they grow best. Unfortunately, the dealers have been giving such rotten prices, and there's been such scandalous profiteering between the wholesale and the retail price, that many country people now utterly refuse to gather the fruit. I know one depot where the chalked-up offer of "½d. per pound" was changed, *after the women had walked there with their loads*, to "4 pounds a ½d." The women were helpless; they could not go elsewhere, so the dealers got away with the haul. And that very evening, returning to town, I found the average shop price 6d. to 8d. a pound. The country people themselves make delicious puddings, jams, wines and jellies from the blackberry, and it is to be wished some of the modern canning and preserving methods could do something more for this delicious fruit.

The scarlet rowan berry is also cooked by some country people, but has a more subtle value against witchcraft.

F

MOUNTAIN FORESTRY

Wood growing properly belongs to the valleys and the hill and down country, but "forestry" is also a mountain industry. Whole hillsides, and small plantations, and derelict quarries, are planted with firs which used to have a ready sale at standard prices and sizes (20-year growth, 50-year growth, etc.) for pit props. These values have changed with the importation of timber from Norway and Sweden, but for various reasons, as for example round mountain lake reservoirs, etc., the replanting of fir-timber makes a very important mountain industry. Small quantities of small quick growth have a comparatively rapid turnover as Christmas trees when near large towns. For ourselves, in the hills, we use the undressed poles for stack centres, barriers, palings in the steadings, and rafters for our slate roofs. By the mountain streams a few alders may be sold "standing" to clog block-cutters. This waterproof wood is considered the best for clog soles. Now that there is much less demand for clogs in the North, these camps of clog sole-makers are few, but on the whole the clog itself tends to become a much better finished article, as the few workers who appreciate, or must of necessity use, clogs will afford the best possible article.

29 DECEMBER ON DARTMOOR: A Halt at 1,500 feet

30   " THE SLUMBERING MIDLAND PLAIN "

CHAPTER III

THE UNDULATING FARMLANDS

" 'Tis strange that no author should have written fully of the fabric of ploughs. Men of the greatest Learning have spent Time in contriving Instruments to measure the Immense Distance of the Stars, and even Weight of the Planets . . . they bestow the utmost of their skill, learnedly to pervert the natural Use of all the Elements for Destruction of their own Species by the bloody art of War. Some waste their whole Lives in studying how to arm Death with new Engines of Horror, and inventing an infinite variety of Slaughter, but think it beneath Men of Learning (who alone are capable of doing it) to employ their learned Labours in the Invention of new, or even improving the old Instruments for increasing of Bread."

TULL, *Principles of Tillage.*
MDCCLI

THIS is England, the real England of peaceful villages and sociable people. Plain England, where cottages cluster round a church, close as chickens to a hen, where buses beetle along the level roads, and there is an atmosphere of unhurried activity. Where farms sit down amid their solid acres, and heavy agricultural machinery works steadily, where the placid passing of the seasons over the undulating fields quietly smooths the passage of the year from Spring to Summer, through Autumn to Winter. Here are none of the great seasonal changes of the mountain heights or restricted valley lands.

This gently undulating or almost level agricultural land comprises, as its largest area, the country covered by that hunting term "The Shires." The "Midland plain" (so-called) is at its most solid around Leicester and Nottingham, where it merges into the wide slow Trent Valley. Eastward, beyond Northampton and into Cambridgeshire, it is at its most quietly charming; westward to Oxfordshire it becomes its most individual. The land changes and shades gradually upwards till it reaches Cotswold, with its stone walls and sheep and villages of satisfying yellow stone, stone which mellows as golden as if it held centuries of warm sunshine. North Oxfordshire is as individual as its strong stone buildings, and as sturdy as its yeoman stock. It has not the wide serenity of open Cambridgeshire, but is subtly complementary. Farther to the east, beyond Cambridge, by Huntingdon and Rutland, this midland region merges into

East Anglia proper. Southwards, the quietly undulating midland plain reaches the Thames Valley through Bedfordshire, North Bucks and a strip of South Oxfordshire, and crosses it into North Berkshire and Wiltshire. Northward and westward it stretches through Warwickshire and North Worcestershire to the hills and moors of the Pennines, with a separate extension taking in North Shropshire and most of Cheshire. In the extreme South-east, the undulating plough and grass lands of Essex must come under the same review; they are perhaps more individual in traditional usage than any other part of England.

Geologically, the "stone" line of oolitic limestone running south-west by north-east through Oxfordshire and Northamptonshire is a well-defined band, but it produces on its lower levels this same type of country (here, however, largely made up of clays, marls, and sometimes even sandstone). Thus, the boundaries of the undulating farmland area are extraordinarily difficult to define; roughly we speak of "The Midlands" or "The Shires," admitting that most of East Anglia has the same undulating character, but excepting certain special localities (for example, the flat individual strip of land behind Selsey Bill, which, though superficially similar to the flat parts of Essex, is utterly unlike *any* other portion of England).

Generally speaking, a pasturage map (that most misleading of all statistical documents) will mark off the entire east coast, including Essex and Lincoln, as "cultivated land," but this does not lift the ploughshare from the green fields of the Midland and West. *It only goes to prove the high percentage of grazing left among the cultivated acres of the Midlands.* The Leicester and other large breeds of sheep and the huge green fields full of cattle mark pasturage; but the alternate fields, as full of corn as a bowl is full of cream, lie among the green. Probably "the country of mixed farming" is the best definition for the undulating Midland plains. Only people living in The Shires realise how characteristically mixed the farming is! Usually "mixed" on each farm, but sometimes locally, one farm and another specialising separately. Corn, roots and stock may be the steady principle, yet, especially near a large market, there will always be most unexpected variations. I remember how one year, near Nottingham, a farmer who had always run the typical successful mixed farm, and whose steady success depended on doing the usual humdrum average rather better than anyone else, suddenly went "all intensive" and covered the landscape with garden peas! His solid field gates nearly came off their hinges with people leaning over them speculating on his sanity. There wasn't a horse gig in the neighbourhood that didn't pull up automatically as the driver registered his astonishment. But those peas were a phenomenally successful harvest. He had to recruit unskilled labour, with difficulty, from an unaccustomed neighbourhood, sending far in farm wagons to collect women and children to pick. Because when the peas turned up a month early, green and juicy, they fairly swept the local market, and sent dozens of plump ducks to a sudden and succulent end! I remember him retailing the story of his "Market Ordinary" dinner in Nottingham, after the weary weeks of press-ganged harvesting. "The waiter, he come breathing over my shoulder, and sets down the plate as careful as china, and smirks 'I've brought you a few *pays*!' says he. 'Green pays!' (and there were nubbut a speuneful!) 'Pays!' I said, 'Pays! I'm fair sick of Pays!' Poor waiter chap he seemed quite taken aback." But the same success did not attend the whimsical purchase of six black-faced sheep that had happened (by what untimely visitation of a Northern God!) to get into the Leicester market. He drove them back one evening in the dusk; next morning those sheep had cleared the fence, and were reared up on end pruning our standard roses! Followed a reign of terror on that peaceful Midland farm. The sheep-dog fled ignominiously, the goats (ordinary placid creatures kept because their milk was supposed to "agree better" with the baby) were fired to emulation, and followed the black-faced sheep over the fence into the yard, where they ate the washing. Being driven out, they then stampeded the milking cows into panic through the local watercress bed; and finally the mountaineers (passing via the poultry corn bin) lightly took a six-foot stone wall into the kitchen garden and ate the brussels sprouts! As the farmer's wife said: "Corn *and* greens they have taken"; and as *he* said, when I passed him driving them back to mid-week market: "Thur devuls, thur devuls." That was the only comment I ever heard him make on the black-faced breed!

It is a queer thing how horses love a donkey in their fields—they will sometimes bite and tease one another, but they are always friendly to their donkeys. It was on this farm that the small donkey who took the odd milk churn to the station three miles off once met his "grazing mate" at a meet, and forthwith abandoned the milk cart and joined the Quorn Hunt! And as the boy driver (who'd been pretty well "milked over in the hedge") remarked: "the little beggar wasn't the last in the field by a long way."

The Midlands of England have a characteristic atmosphere of good solid worth, extraordinarily satisfying and extraordinarily difficult to define. Samuel Butler recommended a course of the "Upper Mammals" for nerves, and for the fretful or weary I would, in all seriousness, suggest a holiday passed between the Rivers Nen and Trent. I know no other part of England where one may travel so far in any direction, so comfortably, without any very great adventure, but with a day of full pleasantness. This level Midland country life is solid, and compared with the changeable seasonal hill life the year moves smoothly as butter! But the months are too full and too varied to be monotonous, and all the year the landscape shows the same quiet continuous unfolding.

Go in summer. There are small winding streams between meadows gold with buttercups, where the cream foam of meadowsweet scents the air, and gold water-lilies float swaying gently. . . . In the green sloping fields drowse cows, lazily flicking flies; the sound of the mowing-machine hums through the air, and the sweet scent of warm hay fills the sunshine. Along the dusty white roads stand bushy elm-trees, whose treachery it is to drop their thick-leaved boughs suddenly in full summer. "The hale old goes sudden as elum boughs" is a local saying. On the first touch of autumn the elm-tree has a single lemon-coloured bough, gleaming among the green. Among the farms, in the dusk of the evening, the howl of the separator is heard in the land, and you turn down some lane with thick flowery hedges and grass growing high between the cart-wheel ruts to a brick-built homestead with red-tiled floors, and have cream, limpid running cream (not the stiff clotted cream of the West, but sloppy yellow cream with bubbles in it) and hot tea-cakes, and eggs, and many, very many, different sorts of jam for tea. In the evening an owl hoots in the elm-tree under your window, a white-brown noiseless ghost crosses the moonlit barn, and the watch-dog rattles his chain and grunts in his sleep.

Brick is the general building material, brick and timber; the gate-posts and gates are of good solid timber, and in the hunting districts they have heavy wooden catches, easy to lift with the hunting-crop. Of stone walls in the fields there are none, but the hedges of the Midlands are miles of delight. There are hawthorn hedges, white and pink, close-set mixed hedges, plashed and laid level, hedges that show the "'ware wire" red tab for the hunters; field corners from which odd shoots may be drawn for repairing a hedge, and sometimes a stray damson-tree, a wild crab-apple, or black hollybush leans over and makes a shade for the young cattle. The hedger is a skilled workman, as skilled as a dry stone dyker of the fells.

31 HEDGEROW ELMS ON THE MIDLAND PLAIN

32   A MIDLAND PASTURE

33   A RIVER PASTURE ON THE SEVERN

The local "billhook," "breasting bill" and hedgeman's long-handled axe vary between one county and the next; any countryman will recognise the handiwork of some special hedge setter for seasons after his job is done. Some of the "road men" who care for stretches of the hedge-bound highway are workmen of great skill. The hedgeman's thick heavy leather glove (the facsimile of those drawn in the early English manuscripts) hangs for sale in all small saddlers' shops among the leather knee-pads, the horse saddles, the very long plough reins and the work-horse collars. Every sort of hedge is to be found dividing up the undulating farmlands; the raised up "dyke hedge" with its drain alongside and its layered and staked fence; the young "protected hedge," with its wire line stretched on either side, or the old forgotten hedge where a wandering line of high gnarled hawthorn-trees stagger across the grazing field, their roots deep-pitted into sandy hollows by sleepy sheep, their sides polished to ivory by generations of rubbing fly-stamping horses. Then in hay-harvest times there is the hedge that is gaily hung with the white wisps from the passing hay wagons. Yes, we must have early summer in the Midlands; and drink great jugs of hot tea, and eat thick bread and butter and cheese and jam in a Midland hayfield, under the hedge.

August in the Midlands hears the binder clattering around the field, the fat sheaves steadily dropping out, and the guns waiting for the rabbits in the last round. Then there is fermity and rabbit pie in the cottages, and the harvest moon rises huge and red behind the elm-trees and sheds red-gold light over the folded hands of the praying corn stooks—the eight-fold stook of wheat, the feathery stooks of the barley and the quivering oats, who of old were supposed to have "three churchings before carrying" (i.e. three weeks in the field)—though now all corn harvesting is much more swift. Nowadays the hay-lift wipes the hay from the field and flings it up into a stack "within three days of the grass," and the threshing machine is panting over the corn, and the chaff bags are filling "before you know it is autumn!" Then, the hens are out in the stubble, the long smoke lines of the burning twitch drift across the fields, there is a bloom on the damsons in the orchard, and the apples are

HEDGER'S
BILLHOOK

ripe. Yellow swedes from the fields and turnips appear on the farm dinner table, the cattle are chewing from the sticky root troughs, and in the cold frost of the fields cows crunch cold white field cabbages, and—it is winter in the Midlands.

Probably because of the proximity of pigs and poultry one seems to eat an awful lot of eggs-and-bacon in the Midlands, and because of unlimited butter and eggs there is a crisp variety of tea-cakes. One gets scones in the North, pikelets in the Pennines, oat cakes on the mountains, muffins south of the Thames, and tea-cakes in the Shires. Each part of England has its special dishes; Melton Mowbray of the Shires has given its name to pork pies, Stilton cheeses are Midland, but more than anywhere else the undulating Midland plains are the warm home of "the Market Ordinary." A Midland market town is a comfortable unhurried sort of place; Nottingham, the largest open market in England, has removed its wooden stalls to more "convenient" quarters, and the whole character of the place has accordingly sadly changed. But all the smaller country markets have the "Market Ordinary." Far on the west, where the Midland plain, passing beyond Shropshire, peters out at the foot of the Welsh hills, is Oswestry market. South-

HEDGER'S LONG-
HANDLED AXE

east is Royston, in the land of the old Stourbridge fairs. Northward is Melton Mowbray, southward is Chipping Norton; and between these outposts, and all around, the Market Ordinary is eaten. Usually the early buses on a market day are full of farm folk and stall-holders; the shoppers follow on the next bus. Any time after eleven the "cars" drive in, and have to "park" (the farmer's traps can stable at the inn); some of the "gentry" may have lunch *à la carte* at the hotel; some weak-minded womenfolk may go to a café and have coffee and buns; unfledged cowboys may go to the stalls and have tea and meat pies, but the majority of people who come into a market town, on a market day, eat a Market Ordinary.

Now the last stronghold of the good old English cooking is in the oven of the "Market Ordinary," and the savour from its grill, if it could materialise a ghost, would produce Mr. Pickwick. A "Market Ordinary" is a large helping of the most popular local product, bought at its seasonal prime in the local market; it is well and plainly cooked in the inn kitchen, and simply and most generously served, on coarse white table-

34 BURNING "SCUTCH" IN THE AUTUMN FIELDS

35 A PLOUGH-TEAM ON SALISBURY PLAIN.
Notice the plough-staff resting between the handles

36 THE RETURN OF THE PLOUGH-TEAM

cloths on long strong tables, 12–3 p.m. The platters may be thick, the knives and forks clumsy, but the food will be good. At an Oxfordshire "Ordinary" I have had saddle of mutton, red-currant or barberry jelly, spinach and potatoes, apple pie and cream, a dish of cheese straws and cider. Near Nottingham for a "Market Ordinary" I have had roast duck and peas, lemon pudding, cream cheese and biscuits (home-made) and excellent Trent Valley ale. East towards Rutland, later in the year, I have eaten roast beef, horse radish, roast potatoes, cabbage, followed by damson tart and custard and Stilton cheese. On the West I have had salmon and Caerphilly, and if you are not sustained sufficiently till you get home you won't have done justice to the "Market Ordinary." Of course, later, you will usually get the local speciality in buns, pies, etc., cleanly served with lavish rural generosity, and mugs of boiling hot tea in the market tea-stall. The Midland country marketer is well sustained!

After market, from three to four, or five or six, the roads out of the town are full of passing traps and cars and cyclists, and the buses, with their steamy windows, are awfully slow getting back, because they have to stop and unload four bundles to each passenger—and the passengers are usually met by two or three children who have been waiting for hours to "help carry the parcels off the bus."

In this land of level wide roads and domestic population, the delivery van supersedes the small "pack pedlar" of the hills and valleys. The conditions make a much larger field possible. Also (the tramp masters of many casual wards will bear me out in this) the small pedlar and trader of the mountain and valley districts sticks to his own *type* of *district* in his journey across country. I have tracked some such pedlars passing from Cardiff, to Birmingham, and on into Notts. They will not take the direct level route, but deviate to follow the hills through Droitwich and Shrewsbury, along the edge of the Peak District, through Derby to Nottingham. In the same way some pedlars follow rivers, venturing reluctantly across the long and wearisome open stretches of the Midlands, so that the latter are characteristically the land of the vehicle trader.

During twenty-five years I can trace the development of one "Onions" whose ramshackle pony trap said:

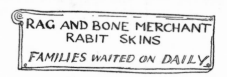

RAG AND BONE MERCHANT
RABIT SKINS
FAMILIES WAITED ON DAILY

(this was because he bought a greengrocery cart second-hand and wasn't good at lettering!) He rattled round exchanging toys and penny mops and small household oddments (in the North it would have been hearthstones) for empty jam jars, ex-rabbit skins and rubbish.

Finding the oddments sometimes sold for more than "exchange," he turned it into a cash concern and clashed around the hedgerows with saucepan lids and brooms and local baskets of willow, made by himself. Presently some enterprising commercial traveller constrained him to deal in coupon soap; later tea towels and enamel ware augmented the newly painted cart. Last time I saw the name it swished by on a large motor lorry with a box-body, let-down sides and a cash till; and you could buy anything from a nutmeg grater to a complete china toilet set, and book your orders as from a departmental store!

Our first fish-cart was less successful, on account of local conditions, because most Midland farm-house *front* doors are glued up for life, except for funerals and weddings, and the fishman had to leave his cart in the street while he went round to the back doors, and the cats would grab the fish. He caught my cat once, and when I came to the rescue he was holding her by the scruff, and flip-flapping her backwards and forwards with a fluke fish (the culprit elongating with miserable resilience). Then he wanted me to buy the fish! But it really was the end when, one Friday before an August Bank Holiday, he speculated in a job lot of mussels which wouldn't sell (they were not a "*known*" fish in our locality; Lancashire likes mussels most). He was angry that nobody would buy this fish, so he had a drink, and then went the entire length of the High Street strewing handfuls of mussels broadcast before the doors, each side. It was three days in the hot sun before the street cleaner was due to come round—and then *he* nearly struck.

The Midlands may be quiet country, but they are never monotonous.

In the undulating farmlands it is extraordinarily difficult to specialise in any one branch of agriculture because, the surface of the country remaining unchanged, the condition of the soil, and very markedly the conditions of rainfall, make for great variation. While the Midlands proper (with their large percentage of pasture-land and meadow interspersed between the cultivated fields) have considerable rainfall, the Eastern district is the driest part of England. This dryness, and the comparative absence of timber, give an

37 MAKING SHEPHERDS' CROOKS IN A SUSSEX BLACKSMITH'S SHOP

38   A FARM GROUP BENEATH THE MALVERN HILLS

39   THE CHEQUER-BOARD OF ESSEX

open spaciousness to the Eastern landscape, absolutely different from the green, somewhat heavy somnolence of the central West area.

The familiar bulge of the extreme East of England, in Norfolk and Suffolk, is the area of the ancient kingdom of East Anglia, and constitutes a district largely self-contained and having a very definite and individual character of its own. Like the Midland area it forms an undulating plain, but that represents the only extent of the similarity. It is otherwise as diverse, both scenically and agriculturally, as it is geologically, though there is a certain amount of boulder clay over both districts.

Norfolk and Suffolk are distinctly drier than the Midlands, for they are swept by strong east winds. Nevertheless, they are perhaps less bleak in character. One factor which helps is that, while there are not very many great areas of woodland in East Anglia, there are many small copses, and the abundant hedgerow timbering gives a woodland pattern among the field chequerwork which is largely absent from the great grass fields of such a district as Leicestershire. There is a delicate charm about the pastoral landscapes of East Anglia, especially in spring along the river valleys, which the early water-colour painters loved. Artists call this part Constable's Country.

It almost seems as though the strongly marked character which pervades East Anglian buildings, and the steadfast, independent race which inhabits them, have also set their mark upon the land itself. It is impossible to do justice to this district in a brief and hasty survey. The point that strikes the observant visitor to East Anglia is the untouched, deeply rural character of the countryside itself, as well as of the villages and small towns, which look in their settled calm as though they had not been disturbed for the last hundred years at least. Occasionally there are fair-sized towns serving wide agricultural districts, but throughout the region it is the small town which is most characteristic and frequently most charming. If East Dereham is a substantial centre, there are plenty of little places such as Hingham and Fakenham dotted over the map of Norfolk, as in Suffolk townlets such as Framlingham, Clare, Lavenham and many another shade almost insensibly into larger villages.

Agriculturally speaking, there are spots in which modern outlook and commercial enterprise shout loudly. But scratch below the surface, and probably you get the most stubborn, stick-in-the-mud, conservative feeling in England. On account of the climate and a high percentage of clear air and sunshine, it is one of the few parts of England where it is really possible to ripen corn satisfactorily. It has been well said that Norfolk and Suffolk did much to provide what were the three staple products of the Englishman's diet—bread, beef and beer. Now the sweetening indispensable to modern life has been added. A prominent cereal crop of Norfolk is barley, though both there and in Suffolk much wheat is still grown. The well-known cycle of Norfolk crop rotation continues to be followed with some fidelity, yet there is much grassland scattered throughout East Anglia, grazed by fine fat sheep and herds of cattle, with such specialised products as the Norfolk turkey, raised in such quantities around Attleborough. The long periods of sunshine and the comparatively dry summers are favourable to the raising of "small" fruit such as currants, gooseberries, etc.: there is one landowner near Thetford who combines a profitable, carefully tended crop of black currants with the growing of a large number of young firs for Christmas trees. East Anglia also supplies a good proportion of the straw-berries grown in England. Suffolk is famous for its pigs and grows a rather larger proportion than the rest of wheat—the arable cultivation is mostly found in that high chalk district of South-East Suffolk which joins Cambridgeshire, Hertfordshire and Essex, where in the rolling chalk downland which spreads itself over parts of all those four-named counties is to be found one of the most extensively arable districts in England. Hence East Anglia has a reputation for being our corn bin. This province was the last stronghold of the aboriginal woad, while flax (now grown again near Sandringham), saffron and a dozen older crops stand out against the green overwhelming flow of sugar-beet which in the last years has changed the colour of East Anglia. Between Suffolk and Essex lay the land of our old farmer historian, Tusser, and his sixteenth-century points of husbandry can be commented upon and discussed along his own ground to-day, quite as reasonably as if they were a modern notebook. Some usages have changed, but much remains unaltered. The Suffolk punch, that short cobby stubborn little horse of great strength and independence, may have lost his figure but he has by no means lost his character.

The open quiet of the Cambridge country is as clear as the air blowing across the Cambridge ploughlands, drying them from bronze to whitish grey. As one recent writer has happily expressed it:[1]

[1] The late T. McKenny Hughes in the *County Geography* (Cambridge University Press).

"Cambridgeshire is like a quiet reserved person, who speaks little to strangers, but is full of wonderful stories for those who have learnt to love her with an intimate knowledge . . . it is the quiet villages, the chalk uplands, with their carpet of fine grass and flowers, the lonely peat and fen lands—vast spaces of changing colour and mood stretching away to the sunset— which are the real Cambridgeshire. . . . To the native of a mountainous country the Cambridgeshire hills are mere rising ground, but everything is relative, and these hills which raise us above the plain into the purer air, have nothing higher east- wards between us and the Ural Mountains. Such must have been Campden's idea in 1607, for though he had travelled in many parts of England he writes: 'Near unto Cambridge on the south-east side there appear aloft certaine high hilles, the students called them Gog Magog Hills.' "

On a spring day of blowing white clouds and chasing shadows, the lighting intensifies the waving undulating character of these eastern uplands, so that in contrast the ploughlands of Essex, close down to the misty estuaries and dykes, seem level. In Essex you get that individuality of method and appliance which is always fostered by isolation; the plough- lands are cut off by the London area from the main South- eastern ploughlands, and the soil has necessitated implements of an utterly different character. The Kentish plough, high and angular and heavy footed as it looks to Northern eyes, has its use in consolidating the under-furrow in Kentish land. The Essex wooden plough could have been shaped nowhere else but on the Essex soils. One of the finest ploughing scenes in England can be watched where the red-brown fields of Essex tilt down to the river, and five or six plough teams will be working together, the white gulls fluttering a pennon behind each team. The farmer who can readily cope with the swiftly changing market, and has sufficient capital behind him to subsidise enterprise, is the successful agriculturalist, *not* the man who works hardest, or even in some cases does the best job of farming! The long jobs of improving and cross-breeding, or winning land under to some special cultivation may miss their reward simply because the slow painstaking effort has missed the market. One can witness this in hundreds of fields, (or in the painstakingly fined wool which is now barely worth the shearing cost) and in a dozen instances where necessary slowness of transference or adoption, or lack of co-ordination, have left acres of small-holdings to be sold off at a hopeless loss to large commercial co-operative concerns who can turn them into a profit.

Thus, for example, when the supply of stable manure, cheaply carried by water to Essex fieldside quays from London stables, was not covered by the price obtained for the corn sent back as return cargo, that light land swiftly suffered, without capital or combined enterprise for lorry-imported winter-feeding stock for manuring. Now, at this moment, there are acres and acres of sugar-beet grown in that district. The top trimming of the beet, which has small sugar content and is lopped off in the field, is eaten by sheep. Potatoes, that standby of Essex, where the main roads lorry them quickly back to the London dinner tables, are clamped in some places only with the light dry earth and the modicum of straw. Farther north, in Suffolk, I have seen loads of bracken from over the border in Norfolk used for clamping. It's rather a jolly gathering, the opening of a potato clamp; usually the men workers fix up a sort of windscreen of hurdles, or rushes plaited through open sheep bars; and sometimes it is sacking that flaps gallantly in the wind and bellies from the bending stakes, as if in emulation of the brown barges tacking down the estuary from Ipswich. The men have large graips (flat pronged forks), or open-work shovels, with which they ladle the potatoes into the sieve, and thence to the sacks that hang on the weighing machine; or elsewhere, are parties of field workers hand-gathering into loose nets. The lorry waits with an "easy all" stance, two wheels in the hedge; and the lorry driver and his mate settle down to a quiet pipe in a sheltered spot before the all-night drive back to Covent Garden.

This district, with its easy access to town, usually grows a fair percentage of market produce; "earlier from the west, quicker from the east" is a disputable saying either side of London. In the spring, you may see more hand-sowing of green kitchen vegetables in Essex than almost anywhere. It may be combined coincidence of time and crop, but in Essex I've often come across old seed dibblers who automatically counted the "step-step; tap-knee down" rhythm as they sowed broad beans; and there are more ante-diluvian outlandish dibbling perambulators forming henroosts in Essex barns than anywhere else I know! Five men sowing beans and one boy refilling the "bags" were covering a field whose banked hedges were blue rime of frost on the north-east side, and posied with primroses on the lee. They might have been doing it in the twelfth century.

The hedges of the undulating farmlands might well define the districts as efficiently as they define their fields. Only in

40   NOSE-BAGS AND BREAD-AND-CHEESE ON AN ESSEX FARM

41   A HEDGE-LAYING COMPETITION IN THE MIDLANDS

42   THE SMOOTH GREY BOLES OF A SURREY BEECHWOOD

isolated districts, such as the neighbourhood of Charnwood Forest "rocks," through the stone line of Northamptonshire, and, of course, on the Cotswolds' edge, are there any stone dykes such as we get in the North or West. Characteristically, the lower alluvial lands have the banked hedge, especially developed in windswept districts. You find this banking everywhere you get a sea wind, for the resulting shelter at the ground surface is useful. In many cases the stone clearing of the field, as in Ireland, seems to have determined the position of the bank, but only in some districts. On top of the bank, the smaller fencing shrubs whinny against the wind, and where the hedge has been let "run" whips of blackberry and wild rose sweep in great curves over and across, until on neglected

AN OLD OVERGROWN BANKED DYKE (SECTION)

ground the original small stone dyke is buried ten feet deep in the centre of impenetrable overgrowth, through the centre of which there sometimes meanders a low wool-hung tunnel, pitted with rabbit burrows, where the sheep have kept a way open for a noonday nap. Where the undulating farmlands tilt down on to the levels, hedges peter out and are replaced by sluices and ditches; and where the uplands sweep wide under the open sky are long clean hedges of utterly different type. Perhaps on the borders of Huntingdon, or along the straight Roman roads of East Anglia, may be found some of the best plashed hedges in England.

A good hedger is a true artist; no two men can work alike, and if you get three or four competing along the same hedge, each may be intent to produce the identical type of height and continuity. Yet when they stand back, the three or four different sections of hedge show an individuality as clear as handwriting. Every hedger chooses his own tools; for dyking and plashing the staking a mallet, hedger's axe, billhook and clasp-knife are taken along. Some workers combine mallet and axe in a heavy-headed strong-handled hedger's axe; others have the staking mallet cup shaped, that can drive over the slanting cut stake on top, or over the edge of a projection lower down. Some workers shape the stakes that they cut from the hedge, planning their

spacing out well ahead, while others seem to have an uncanny fore-sighted method; they will flap a wrinkled weather-wise eyelid along the straggling hedge, with a searching glance that flaps, as a bird might, through the branches; then spit, look up at the sky, watch the hunt passing in the distance, pass the time of day with someone on the road, and placidly proceed with their work down the hedge, unerringly numbering out an evenly regulated supply of selected stakes, apparently on the memory of that one comprehensive first glance. If you want to prove this, ask an old hedger for a stake of certain dimensions or shape. He will walk ahead and lay his hand on it at once, and few of the older hands who have been hedging longest can explain this incredible visual memory, more than by the statement that "they noticed how the hedge stood before they began laying it."

HEDGER'S
STAKING
MALLET

The low close hedge up to three or four feet high is built to confine stock, and may have a single fence or wire run along one side of it for some years. The low continuous hedge (with fenced corners for shade) is more common on the mixed farm; the field hedge, very low and close clipped, that runs between crops, is thick-set and, in the best fields, kept clear at the roots and level at the sides, so as not to waste space on the head-lands. The twelve to four-teen feet high hedges be-long to the treeless and rather drier fields of the east; they are the most difficult hedge of all to keep in order, as they

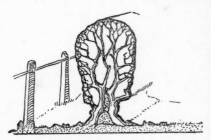

PROTECTED STOCK HEDGE

always tend to "get away" overhead, and to thin out below. The overhang is set free, just clear of grazing stock. Horses are notorious hedgecombers, and can usually be counted on to clip off any superfluous overhanging reach. The long-handled (up to six feet) "bill" of the hedger is used with an upsweep; the sickle varies according to locality (and astonishingly more according to locality and usage than according to type of herbage). The sickle is used in connection with the hooked stick, or with a single cutting sweep. Along some of the thick flowery, grass-swept hedges of Oxfordshire, where Queen

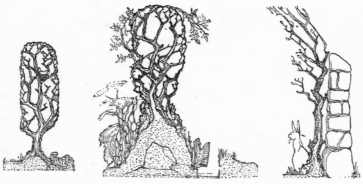

FIELD HEDGE   BANKED HEDGE AND DITCH   HEDGE, DYKE

Anne's lace (cow parsley) stands up, the hooked stick is used with something of the action of the fifteenth-century Hainault scythe to press back the grass, while the sickle slices up from the root and hauls out in level swathes.

Cattle and milk churns both belong to the Midland pasture country of mixed farms. Years and years ago, a town baby came to stay at our home in the Midlands. "How nice! fresh milk for the baby, straight from the farm." So, devoted each morning, I cycled up to the pleasant farm on the green hill while the blue-grey dawn frost still lay on the grass, past the blossoming

SHADY PASTURELAND HEDGE

hawthorn-tree, to where a dozen or more cows stood quietly in the open hay-scented shed. . . . Then came the swish and ring of white foam, milking steadily into the freshly rinsed pails. . . . The pouring of the white warm milk through the milk syle, a careful tilt, and I carried my scalded pannikin of fresh milk swinging on my cycle handle-bar back to the

H

babe, all pure, warm, fresh milk from the farm. Unfortunately, one morning, being delayed (what bird's nest lured me from my devoted punctuality?), I did not wait for the syle, but crouching down by the milkman's three-legged stool, pressing my towzled head against the warm woolly red cow, I caught the warm milk stream direct into my gurgling resonant tin, and fled, hay stranded, back to the nursery. Alack! two strands of the hay caught within that milk-can! The milk "was dirty"! It had been found "full of straws". . . . In the future, coming back from school, I must buy and carry with me some clean pure milk from an approved dairy in town.

So, at eight o clock, I trailed my school bicycle behind the ancient milk float that carried the churn of milk from that same farm to the station. That milk churn and I travelled up by the same train to the hated town, where at the black and noisy depot I saw that same milk churn (did not the homely name on the side strike wistfully to my heart, trudging "like snail unwillingly to school") tilted into the white enamelled brass-bound co-operative milk tank. I remember being friendly with the porter, who reached in and scooped a chipped railway saucer full of milk out of it for the station cat, on the quiet. I watched that morning's farm milk trundled down the road to the white-tiled dairy shop, and that evening, after school, I brought that same milk back with me in a bottle; but *now* it had a stopper on the top, and writing round the sides! So—ten and a half hours later, pedalling past the very cow it had come from that morning, past that very same open hay-scented shed, I returned with the same milk. And reading the labels on the bottle they now said, with satisfaction: "Ah, *this* is Guaranteed Pure Fresh Milk straight from Our Own Dairy. 2d. payable on bottle." . . . Such is the power of advertisement.

That is more years ago now than I care to think about; hopeless then to argue with grown-ups. To this day it seems hopeless to argue with grown-ups—there are the facts, but people will still only use such facts as they think "look nice" in farming.

Perhaps nothing has changed more rapidly with the availability of transport than the milk round. The morning rattle and bang of the heavy milk floats driving the clustered churns to the nearest rail-head has ceased in most districts. It was always an obvious point for co-operation; there would be twenty or thirty floats rattling and racing each other every morning to

43, 44   THRESHING IN SURREY

45 CARTING THE WINTER FEED ON A SURREY FARM

pull up and wait at the station till the train came in. Then the empty churns were collected and driven back, each to be washed separately at each separate farm, usually just at the most inconvenient time of the day when all hands were wanted elsewhere. From the woman's household point of view, the direct selling of milk, not milk products, has altered life completely. All along the English roads are now milk-lorry platforms, and the number that are built from old railway sleepers is allegorically significant! The platforms are a compromise between the height of the milk float that brings the churn, and the height of the lorry that carries it away. The lorries are diverse, but the diversity of the milk float is phenomenal. Most large farms abut on to the high road, and have their own stand close to the lorry round, but the farms farther away get their milk to the stands in the most extraordinary assortment

of vehicles that could surely be collected on one small island! On the level roads an old open-back float may jerk along behind a horse; a light Ford farmer's wagon may cough up a dozen and spin off with a "honk"; a solitary churn may bob along in a side-car, lovingly embraced round the bends by the motor-biker's arm

MILKO!

(a country idyll); mincing along, neat-foot, may come a donkey, deposit the churns and take the children on to school. Up in the mountains, over the narrow stony roads, the churns bump and slide down on sledges; and once on an exceptionally high pasture I encountered a churn sliding down luxurious as Cleopatra, on a couch of ling, which had ingeniously been bedded on to a hurdle for an emergency transport. On some of the high pastures during the spring and summer the milk is carried down in great churns strapped with broad leather straps on to the man's shoulders (the cows having been milked on the open moor-foot grazings). These small dribbles of milk from the far corners contrast oddly with the huge glass-lined tanks which cruise down arterial roads, liners of milk, but it's the small craft that can get into the corners! The cheese and butter industry is passing entirely out of the farmhouse and into the factories, and yet, curiously, there is the same mixture of mass production and individual idiosyncrasy in separating the cream from the milk and in churning.

Nowadays, all over the undulating Midland plain, far across to East Anglia, down to Devon and up through the green valleys of the Northern mountains, the howl of the mechanical "separator" is heard in the land. Yet the West still "clots" its cream. I could name a dozen Midland farms where they still "set it" in shallow pans and skim it with a shell. (The shells may be now a thin-rimmed saucer, but there are still found a few of the fluted draining skimmers.) It is a pleasant sight watching milk being skimmed, the rich cream gathering up into thick leathery folds before the edge of the shell, and falling in heavy soft blobs into the cream pan. Contrariwise, on some farms they still use this method, and will cheerfully wash and scald as many as eighteen shallow milk pans daily, and refuse to "fuss about with the machinery of the separator"; but they make their butter in the most up-to-date of modern churns! Obviously it is not always a question of expense in apparatus.

SKIMMING SAUCER

In some farm households, where the most perfect motor-run "separator" whines and howls in the dairy, the butter may still be beaten up by hand in the most primitive and earliest method. This is especially so in the West, and Devon butter has a good name.

The use of animal power in churning was legislated against, but I know of dogwheel churns running to-day. And under the conditions where they work, "dog churning" seems a very convenient method. The "two-dog-power churn" that I know best operates on the average twice weekly. The two dogs are always hanging round expectantly beforehand, and the minute the door is opened, up they jump on to their wheel, the farmer's wife fastens their collars to the beam above, gives the wheel a starting twist, and off they go, running away for dear life. . . . Presently, pink tongues hang out and they begin to pant, and, with a funny little jump, change legs and speed and trot along till "first stop," when they sit down firmly, tongues hanging out, and get the expected bowl of milk as a refresher. While she clears the churn they lap it up, lick their lips, and then turn round, and wait "ready," settling their legs against the rim boards; another shove and whish! on they go, till presently the wooden wheel begins to trundle uneasily, "bump, bump," the butter is beginning to come in the churn. The dogs know it as well as the dairy wife; you see them pause, look towards each other, perhaps redouble their efforts as if to say "Come on, Bill, give her a quick spin now." . . . lump! lump! . . . "Now, let her rip, ah! easy all, that's done it!";

then they sit down breathless and satisfied, and wait to have their collars undone, when they at once jump down, shake and trot straight to the back door to collect their wages, and—as you might say—"the rest of the day's their own." They obviously *like* the job—running is good exercise—and they thrive on it. Of course, like all animal performances, animal churnings were open to abuse, and I am heartily glad never to have found one of the old "donkey" churns working. For these did not

"TWO-DOG-POWER CHURN"

exploit a natural action, like running. The unfortunate donkey or pony was shut into a box, which balanced across a knife-edge rocker. When the pony's weight was on his front feet, the rocker was down, to the right; when his weight was on the back feet, it tilted back and the rocker was down to the left, and thus, boxed up, the continuous see-saw backwards and forwards continued, and if by any chance the pony contrived staple equilibrium for one second, a slight shove on the box perforce sent him off rocking again. No, it's astonishing what the domestic animal will do for us, but I cannot picture any pony going into one of those rocking boxes willingly!

Of course, the old horse wheel is utterly different and still in common use, where they don't run to a small oil engine; it's the simplest applicable power to hitch on the chaff cutter, or turnip slicer, or small thresher, or any odd job wanted. There are hundreds of types of churns in use in England; the box-wheel churn still sweeps round pretty steadily in some country districts, but it's in Ireland that the dasher goes up and down to the "Hail, Mary!"

The making up of butter has changed according to fashion. Obviously long rolls and compact brick-shaped pieces are easier for transport than the old round-shaped "pounds" that were moulded in round wooden bowls. One small thing that has been lost in the transformation is the individually carved stamp of this bowl, or its cover. The stamps can still be bought chiefly in country shops, because a few small farmers still sell in this rounded form, as do the rather "arty" rural resurrectionists that cluster near cathedral cities. The stamps used to be the characteristic hall-mark of the farm's produce, and were often carved symbolically. Sheaves of corn would show a mixed farm, including cultivated land; sprays of sweetgale a mountain pasture; a swan in rushes a valley farm; or a specially known prize cow would win wooden im-mortality through hundreds of but-ter-gold medallions in the market-place of her old home! I suppose these old hall-marks weren't worth preserving? They had to be scrubbed and cleaned, but then everything connected with the dairy still has to be scrubbed and cleaned. The cor-

BOX-WHEEL CHURN

BUTTER-STAMP

rugated butter "hands" are still with us, and flap designedly over our square blocks, but they have not the individuality of the old carved patters.

The salting of butter follows fashion rather than necessity. Here in the South, when I ask for salted butter, the shop-keepers with a withering glance suggest margarine. Yet many a time a fellow customer, perhaps recognizing a Northern burr

46　A PLOUGHING COMPETITION IN THE THAMES VALLEY

47   THE NOONDAY PAUSE IN A DORSET HARVEST FIELD

in my speech, has joined with me in regret that the fresh "salt tang butter" has gone. The old butter that was salted down for preservation was pretty strongly salted, being strewn with salt as it was knuckled down into casks, and the salt was tremendously controversial for quality. At Droitwich they were said to make a "wonderfully pure salt that excelled the best Dutch salt obtainable," but in those days nothing was put to the salt "than may-be no more than the palm of your hand of soap, to a vat that would bath a beast overhorn, but now, they've took to purifying the salt scientifically, so they don't like it so much!" (O England!) I think it is accurate to say that nowadays salt is a matter of taste rather than of preservation. "Pure, unsalted country butter" perhaps sounds more rural than the "slightly salted." Some of the coarse, highly salted butter, made from somewhat ill-assorted pastures in certain mining districts, is actually preferred as "having more flavour." But many of us only used the unsalted for special sorts of cookery, or jam foods, and liked the slightly salted for all oatcake, cheese, bread or ordinary use; compared to it the unsalted seems insipid.

Beistyn, the milk from the cows soon after calving, is used locally (especially so perhaps in the Midlands) to make delicious custards and curd cakes. It must not be sold, but custom usually sends jugs of it as gifts to the farmers' friends and customers. Superstition says that you must never wash out the jug before returning it, but put in something, if it is only a pinch of salt, an egg or a leaf from the kitchen window plant, to ensure the cow will continue to be fertile. (In the North you must never loan a cradle empty, or return it empty, but to rock an empty cradle is the surest way to fill it!)

The calves are kept separately in the calf house in even the smallest Midland farms (elsewhere I've seen the Irish idea of muzzling adopted, the poor little things looking very mournful, with green plaited willow thimbles over their noses, or buried in tin pannikins!). Hanging derelict on hooks in old cow byres are leather nose straps, with an old cow's horn passing through, that used to be strapped to the calves' muzzles at weaning time, an incredibly dangerous and obsolete method of weaning that must have damaged the udders of many cows. Calves get their milk out of a pail or trough pretty easily, and the milkmaids' fingers at the bottom of the pail are encouragement enough for beginners to suck.

The sale of milk and the factory production of "milk products" should give more people better food. So if in any of these notes my love of the old misleads my admiration for the new, it is perfectly unintentional. Any sort of commercial enterprise, any modernising which makes for better conditions for country workers and cheaper food in town is good, and any co-operation or enterprise which will increase the output of a really British commodity has my last drop of blood—and ink; but going about the country quietly, in a hundred places one finds the first advantage of production on a large scale almost counterbalanced by the later loss of individuality, and lowering of the standard of the product, in order to make a larger output more commerically remunerative. Everyone knows the pleasure of individuality. "Ah! this is home made, it tastes different from what you get from a factory." "Now this is the real thing, this is straight down from the farm," etc. This is not always true or accurate as a value criterion; in some cases the factory article may be actually better, more cleanly produced, have a higher nutritive value, and be in every way the superior product, but in many cases when the product is taken from the hands of the individual, *it is run to make money only at the loss of standard.*

Actually much of the glorified new cheese is really nought but the very old-fashioned "poor house" cheese (pan cheese they call it), that poor folk used to make from the butter-milk, after the butter had been sold separately. They would warm it, curd with rennet, and press and work it with salt, add perhaps a tiny knob of butter to soften it, and shape it up so that it turned out after a month or so, as a smooth stiff cheese, "with which a hard-up chap could fill his wame." Unfortunately, the farmers now see how foolish it is for them to go on making *really good cheese* with their milk when a "commercial chap with a lot of talk" could sell first the cream, and then some butter, and "*then* get just as much for what's left!" So another English cheese loses its fine quality and prestige, and becomes another name in that mass of mediocre stuff with which we try to compete against the foreigner.

There used to be a different sort of cheese for every district in England. Stilton is, of course, the renowned Midland cheese. Gloucester is the valley cheese; Cheshire cheese used to be whitish, and fairly soft (what comes to London is chiefly yellow and hard now); Wensleydale of the right sort, made from the fresh spring grass and delicately blued to mould, is known to a few people as one of the standard best cheeses of England, very individual, something like Stilton, but more delicate. Suffolk cheese had an evil name: "those that made me, were uncivil; they made me harder than the Devil, knives won't cut me, fire won't light me, dogs bark at me, but can't bite me." The ewes were milked in the original makes of this cheese.

Cambridgeshire has its own cheese, Leicester makes individual cheeses, but Nottingham and district on the whole go in with Stilton. Of the South-West, Wiltshire cheeses uphold a good name ('twas in these parts they tried to rake the cheese out of the pond under the yellow harvest moon!). In Somerset, the first cheeses are still baptised in the town stream, and the cream and soft milk cheeses of the West sigh smooth and bland over the white cheese cloths in the country market. Bideford sells a very good creamy cheese. A queer compromise between the milk and cream cheeses used to be made near Lough-

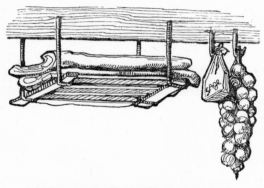

BACON FLITCHES UNDER THE RAFTER

borough. It was called a "tea" cheese, being a milk cheese with a small round cream cheese dropped in its middle like a poached egg. Milk cheeses drained on rush are found in many of the mountain farms. Caerphilly is a flattish white Welsh cheese, and there are scores of small cheeses bearing local names and upholding local reputations, each varying slightly. It will be a pity if these cheeses are all swamped by mass production at a few large centres.

It is difficult to locate the ubiquitous pig, because pork belongs variously all over England. The variety of our British pig is astounding! The upholders of the various breeds each consider their pig THE pig. Besides these pigs, which are THE pigs, there are "pigs" . . . hardy little mountaineers. In life they quarry the hillside behind their mountain farm, after Christmas their lean sides sparkle salt in the lamplight on the rafters above the kitchen table, and their athletic hams dry in the smoke of the chimney corner. Good useful pigs! whose

I

excellent entrails support the family larder, and whose pure white lard oozes into the medicine chest, and flakes the Sunday piecrust. A blessing be on all such good pigs! At Melton Mowbray the shrine of "pig" is shaped like a pork-pie. It was near Melton that a local expert came in to teach us how to disintegrate pig into pork and its essential parts. We had him from Mr. J., "who is very honest for a butcher." He had been fed at a mill, was neither vulgar, big, nor meanly small, but a nice lean, sizeable pig, that would "cut handsomely." First, his sides were laid down for bacon, the spareribs therefrom made boney pie, the hams, so skilfully cut, were sugar-cured by a treasured recipe. The head and trimmings and ears made brawn, the fry was a day's dinner; the sausage meat went into its skin; and the porkpie meat, strewed with seasoning, went into its deep panshon. Then the porkpie crust was made. Boiling water and lard were poured into the warm flour, in

PIE-MOULD

frothing dusty cascades (I can see our experienced little instructor now! big white apron around her middle, lips tightly pursed, the little collar of her dress loosened at the throat, her sleeves rolled up well above the elbow, and her face getting a little pink, as she pummelled briskly up and down, swaying to the resilience of the pliant dough). Then, as the pieces were cut off, they were "raised" round our wooden pie-moulds, with swift admonishing pats and pokes, and little anxious indrawings of the breath, and a satisfactory little snort that put the cooling paste aside to set. Then came the "filling" with sage-powdered peppered pork, the putting on of the lid, and crimping up its edge; the few cut leaves were moulded with the caress of a master hand upon the rounded top, the little hole in the middle was made to let out the steam, and finally the round white pie was entrusted to the depths of the big brick oven. When the pies came out, the gristle of pig and trimmings which had been boiled to a thick savoury jelly were skilfully poured in through that little top hole to fill the encircling cavity left where the pie crust had baked clear of the filling. (Those were *good* pies! any pig might have been proud to be in pies like that!) The lard was rendered down in a big iron pot, just as in the mountains they render down the mutton fat. As the clear transparent oil was ladled from the pot to cool, whitening in the deep jars, the little bits of skin (flead), dried and brown, fried crisp, these "scratchings," as they called them, were scratched up

48   THE FUN OF THE FAIR

49   THE SADDLE-TREE MAKER

50   THE BINDER AT WORK IN DORSET

from the bottom of the pan, sprinkled with chopped parsley and eaten for breakfast, or made into "scratchy pastry," this last a variant of the beaten flead cake of Kent. The brawn was turned out, glassy and cold to the mustard, and long after the "soft meat" (as they called the pork that was eaten at once) had vanished, we remembered Him (studded with cloves and bristled with crumbs before the fire); as curls of bacon, for breakfast, or warmly, in "lardy cakes," at teatime. So end all good English pigs according to their breed.

Re English Eggs and Bacon. Hens like to get together with a loose pig, because he's such a good forager. He digs, they hang round and peck. It's illegal to have a pig unringed if he digs about too much and damages, but a pig loose around, where there are hens about, is an economic proximity which ends at the breakfast table.

Everywhere in England they keep hens, ducks, geese, and sometimes turkeys, with occasionally a guinea fowl (in the river valleys swans). Some "keep poultry," others "poultry farm." Throughout England the number of hens is very unrestricted, ranging from a sad couple shut into a backyard, to two thousand loose in a pen. On the whole, the spacious poultry farm spreads most openly over the undulating plains, though there are notable exceptions, and the Sussex poultry farms are excellent.

Any mixed farm has, as a rule, a mixed breed of hens, who rove about the farm steading and cluster up at the appointed place at breakfast and teatime. This is not considered a "good way" to keep hens, but it's non-proven that their egg output is noticeably less than those of better regulated poultry. As in all farming, so much depends on the individual. A lot of lazy nondescript hens, snooping round, are no credit to anyone, but some diligent domesticated "fair layers" are all to the good. Sometimes their pedigree is known but mixed, at other times this sort of hen is called "barn-door" to prevent further enquiry.

The economic aspect of the "barn-door" hen is hotly condemned by some poultry experts, but in practice they don't do so badly. Their individual behaviour is known to their egg-collecting owner, and ones that do not pay become "nice boiling fowls" next market day. Barn-door hens often have a proper henhouse, but mostly they lay in odd places, and usually the farm children collect the eggs "after school" regularly, making a round of stable, disused loose box, bottom of cartshed, corner of haystack, shelf above the cornbin, or wherever convenient custom among their hen community has decreed the egg shall be laid. Incidentally, if a hen has made up her mind she'll lay in any one special place, you'd have to resort to physical violence to prevent her doing it! She'll snoop round, and cawk about for hours, scrabble up a wall, or sneak under a loose board, but if she has set her mind on one special place, she'll make a dead set for it, and (as when dealing with most limited mentalities), you had better let her have her way.

When a barn-door hen goes "broody" it lies between her owner and her temperament. Some hens let the farmer's wife fuss around, and fix them a nest, and put down bracken and wire netting against the rats, and pepper against the vermin, and sacking against the draught, and rue against the witches, and wait for the moon to get into the right quarter; and then they are given the selected eggs, and "set" upon them in a proper box. And thereafter that sort of hen expects to be "lifted off" and fed very solicitously, and, getting near chipping time, perhaps the eggs have to be sprinkled with a little warm water in case the shells have got too hard, etc. That is usually a *Special* hen. But one of more genuine barn-door ancestry often sneaks off and lays her own eggs and keeps quiet about it, and if she escapes foxes and weasels, turns up proudly with maybe twenty chickens fluffing round her brood-stiffened legs. It is notorious that the hen who acts thus usually brings off a particularly successful brood.

One independent old lady I knew brought off twenty-four chicks absolutely unsuspected in a thorn clump close to a busy highway, but what gained that hen honourable pension for life were the mangled carcases of three large rats found just outside the rim of her nest; each rat had been slain by one shrewd driving blow downwards, severing the cervical vertebrae. She must have faced round while sitting, and quietly waited till the rat was almost underneath her, to deliver that one powerful downward blow. Now *she* was an individual hen. Mostly broody hens are awfully idiotic and exasperating. It would be an education to any pullet, to see a good brooder arranging her nest, making constructive little dabs at the nest straw, pulling up the sides, waggling her feet, and turning and tucking the eggs under her capable bosom, all the time making small scolding placating noises, and finally subsiding into maternal inertia. All eggs in a sitting don't chip out at the same time, so most farmhouses in brooding time have a round basket with a fold of blanket on top waiting in the fender. There's nothing so peaceful as an empty farmhouse kitchen some cold spring afternoon, the dinners all cleared away, the place swept up and polished, the fire burning quietly in the wide stove and that quaint "cheeping—cheeping" like a smothered cricket, coming out of the basket in the corner.

I've never known anyone able to resist that song of spring. Very far away, in a kitchen at Rondavel in Rhodesia, I heard that sound. "Ku-ku?" I asked, and two huge black pink-palmed hands gently produced the little yellow "Kana, ka Nkuku" from the back of the tin oven. "He sing Cheefire so ver' loud!"

A "Poultry Farm" is more like an egg factory. Some Midland farms are most scientifically efficient; usually each farm specialises in one or more notable breeds and methods. There are most ingenious mechanical gadgets for feeding, sorting and gritting with automatic seed hoppers. There are weighing machines and dust baths, and the number of eggs are ancestrally accounted for by trap nesting. In fact, a fowl ceases to have any private life and becomes a regulated paying proposition.

This wire-enclosed world has its own requirements and conditions, grows its own corn, hatches its own eggs, dresses its own "birds," markets its own poultry and purifies its

SITTING HEN, BARN-DOOR BREED

own feathers (offal and guano usually stay on the land). Large poultry farming of this sort is a very specialised industry. Its incubated chicks turn to a curtain-hung and lamp-warmed tin hen, and cluster around galvanised brooders, and the posting of day-old chicks in special padded boxes is a regular duty. "Poultry" more and more tends to become a commendable commercial proposition, but it does seem rather mean to trick the hens into laying overtime by switching on the electric light in the middle of the night! Certainly poultry farming for fresh eggs and spring chickens seems to be an English industry worth developing, but the transition from domestic hen to commercial incubator needs skilful adjustment. I knew one small family who had to start in and eat off one hundred and forty-four hard-boiled eggs the first try.

All over the undulating farmlands, not only in the Eastern Counties where the dry weather and high percentage of sunshine make corn-growing a possibility, but also in the more unsuitable western parts of England, there will always be a certain amount of corn-growing. Apart from quotas and fluctuating markets, there seems to be nothing that quite takes its place in the land rotation. Manure is always a problem, nothing yet replaces the organic manure of the steading, and for this straw is needed; so the corn for the poultry farms may be bought foreign-imported, or it may be grown on land which requires the bringing-in of a corn crop. The loose-boxes of the hunters will still rustle with straw. Straws will stick between the builders' bricks, trundling along for the new Council houses. Sussex oats (a special mixture of grain peculiarly ground in the husk) are used for fattening Sussex poultry, and have a considerable reputation. Incidentally, they make an excellent porridge, the best you can get in the South.

Always there will be, surely, many fields of yellow corn in England's green and pleasant Midland, and so long as a grain grows in England, so the old scarecrow will stand to his weather-beaten duty under the dusty elm-trees of the undulating Midland farmlands.

51 A RIPENING WHEAT-FIELD. There are still a few left, thank God, to pattern our green

52 THE RICH VALLEY GROWTH OF SOUTH DEVON:
A Cottage near Blackpool

CHAPTER IV

GARDEN AND ORCHARD COUNTRY

"Hear hills do lift their heads /aloft from whence sweet /
    springes doe flow;
Whose moistvr good doth /firtil make the valleis /covchte
    belowe.
Hear goodly orchards /planted are in frvite /which doo
    abovnde
Thine ey wolde make their /hart rejoyce to see /so pleasant
    grovnde!"

> From a sixteenth-century map of the Shires
> of Worcester and Warwick woven in tapestry
> by Richard Hyckes.

THERE are small folds in the hills, whose sloping sides
catch the sun, and whose bottoms shelter a little house and
garden, or perhaps a meadow with a few cows. These are an
epitome of the larger river valleys between the mountains
where, sheltered from the wind, sloping hillsides catch the
sun, and wide rivers have waved smooth green levels below.
According to the direction of the valley for the sun and the
wind, and according to the soil, there will be specialisation of
crop and industry.

The valleys of Kent and Hampshire are good examples of
highly specialised districts, largely concentrating on cultivation
of the hop. The wide Wharfedale valley of rich meadows and
upland grazing is a good example of another kind of specialising, as the Wensleydale cheese proves. The great Severn valley
of orchards is a type of the fruit and vegetable growing
districts. The small level coastal strip south of the Solway
Firth, up which the wet sea wind blows, is another variety.

As the type of valley differs, so does the life and work of
the local folk differ, even more markedly than on the mountains,
for the outline of a valley is often very distinct, and a hill
range will constitute the border of one district from another
markedly different. Thus it is that the river valleys are notably
individual in everything, so that to pass from one valley, over
the hill-top down into another, is to change country completely. The work in a valley, with its definitely prescribed
areas, and centralising drainage system, is utterly different from
the work of the open.

Let us take the long deep Western vale of the Severn. It begins as a stream down a crack in the Welsh hills, and opens out into an estuary at Bristol. You can trace the most perfect sequence of valley life and industry all down the valley of the Severn. There are two definite times of the year to send visitors here, either when the fruit is ripe in the autumn, or at the loveliest time of the year, in the spring. Then, far on the west side of the valley, the Welsh hill barriers are still covered with the melting winter snow, and the swift streams are rushing down fresh, white and cold. All the wet green vale sparkles and shines, moist with drifting rain, and the grass has a feathery soft quality and the sheen of living emerald. Overhead in the blue sky the torn white banners of the rain clouds trail out from the Western mountains, and the swift spring sunshine pours down the tilted hillsides, in almost tangible, straight-edged shafts. If ever the crock of gold is found it will be on an April morning in the Severn valley, for there, arch over arch, the rainbows span the valley lands, and spill down translucent waterfalls of colour through the budding trees.

A month later the fruit trees will be in full blossom—white fruit blossom in the Vale of Evesham (53) below the brown line of the Western hills, and then the long winding valley, filled with white blossom either side the silver Avon!—you may see it from the edge of Winchcombe Hill, and follow the line of the edge northward for miles.

There is fruit blossom all over country England in spring, but it blossoms at its most delicious fragrant best where it drifts in soft foam down the green and silver valleys. The plum-blossom, so frail and light; the pear-blossom, so cold and pure, its silver green claws holding the same curve that the honeysuckle will hold later on; the apple-blossom, pink shell'd and fragrant, and the loose, lovely laughter of bronzed cherry —the softest sweetest bloom of all.

In Kent valleys are the largest cherry orchards, but the wilding cherries grow high up in the narrowest hill valleys of all, even where they cease to be valleys, and peter out in cracks up the hillside:

> "And since to look at things in bloom,
>   Fifty springs are little room
>   About the woodlands I will go
>   To see the cherry hung with snow."
>
>   A. E. HOUSMAN, *The Shropshire Lad*

Hey! for a spring day, too long gone by, up by the clear brown youth of the Severn, fresh and cold from the hills, the

53   WORCESTERSHIRE APPLE-ORCHARDS IN SPRING

54   HORNER : A Somerset Village in its Orchard Tangle

new clear sunshine touching the green pastures and waking the primroses on the tilted banks. The air was full of bloom, soft yellow dust of the catkins, but yet the green mosses under my knees were deep spongefuls of winter rain, and flood water glinted through the grass blades. . . . Winter and spring were meeting high up in the river valley! The air was liquid with bird calls, and the silver splashing of cold water. . . .

A cold breath of wind, less a breeze than a little shiver in the air, came down the valley, changing for an instant the silver note of the myriad little waterfalls, and shaking a patter of drifted raindrops from the willows. . . . In the small quiet,

SPRING IN THE VALLEY

after the wind, came a scent, faint, aromatic and indescribable. . . . it was the scent of fresh wet cherry-blossom. . . . Then as water and air took up their silver song again, a white drift of blown cherry petals drifted past, floating down the brown river. . . . So, it held, the Spring Song of the Upper Severn, the silver of the water, the chill of the wind, fresh scent of the blossom and the white petals drifting down the river.

Below, where the valley opened out, the stilt-legged new lambs were wobbling about in the orchard, and the white spring washing of the farmer's wife was flap, flapping on the clothes line.

The typical timber and plaster of the Border houses keep their orchard colouring all the year, for the gay gardens and straw-thatched bee-skeps hold every colour of the rainbow from April to September, and the houses are often colour-washed

K

bright pink, pale yellow or clear blue—it is "garden and orchard" country—and the grim guardian castles of the Border stand up over it, as armed knights must have stood dark above the flower gardens of their ladies.

In the central vale by Hereford, to Somerset in the south, and Monmouth in the west, spreads the cider country. The cider orchards of the West are, some of them, very, very old, and incredibly dilapidated; some are hung with grey moss and thick with mistletoe—theoretically disgraceful, but a joyous pink eiderdown in the spring, and unaccountably prolific in the

BEE-SKEPS, OLD STYLE AND NEW

autumn. The new, correctly planted cider orchards are managed infinitely better, and are in every way commendable, and they will continue, increase and spread, for the makers of cider have ever been devoted to their job; down the cider records for centuries the planters prove that they have spared no pains, nor time, nor money in finding, importing, transplanting, crossing and in every way preserving and improving the cider apple mixtures. Yet, we hope, up round the smaller farms there will always be a few of the small, old friendly orchards, hopelessly unregulated, disgracefully abandoned and therefore most incomprehensibly prolific. On these old farms the wooden cider mill creaks yearly round, and the clear cider flows from the press, turned by half a dozen friends, and the old horse clomps round and round, steadily, as steadily as the arguments creak round and round as to whether this year's

55 PLUM-BLOSSOM AND HALF-TIMBER IN THE VALE OF EVESHAM

56 A LITTLE BRIDGE NEAR WICKHAM MARKET, SUFFOLK

57 GREEN SUMMER ON THE RIVER MOLE, near Dorking

58   SURREY WOODLAND

59   KENTISH COMMON

60   A DOWNLAND FARM NEAR WEST DEAN, SUSSEX

61   A HOMESTEAD IN THE BRENDON HILLS, SOMERSET

vintage "will be as good as last," or, "more like the year when so-and-so, or such-and-such," and how the "old horsehair mat is beginning to wear" (clomp! clomp!), they "might have to come down to coir" (clomp! clomp!)—and the old horse (clomp! clomp!) goes on round and round, and the brown pumice squelches in the stone trough. Sometimes one feels that this is how cider *should* be made, as a peaceful family job among ourselves. They say the monks of Glastonbury were the fathers of English cider; after the sun-warmed wines of the South, our English drinks must have wrinkled the roofs of their mouths, and our honey-warmed mead is more typically a drink of the undulating cornlands than of the fruit-bearing valleys. In the Southern cider country, the apple pulp is packed up with straw into the press, and there beginneth the age-long argument between the two methods. The straw users contend that there "is a power of minerals raised up out of the soil into all grass, and the apple juice is searching acid and brings it out" and so cider obtains real improvement from the use of straw, oat straw for preference. They point out that the quality of the straw does definitely affect the cider, and condemn the blanket wrappers of the North. They, in turn, contend that their cider is clearer, and doesn't "lose its acid to the straw," and both districts drink vast quantities to prove their opinions.

Perry is also made, but the staple drink of the West is cider, as the staple drink of the East is beer. Old recipes show an extraordinary amount of imagination in cider-making, and some local vintages still continue to "make up" these hogsheads by old recipes. Characteristically, cider makers of the Devon valleys used to put milk, eggs and cream into their cider, and the Cornish miners used sheep's blood (hot!); Kent cherries, blackberries and spices went into cider, and the natural gum that oozed from the trees was used instead of the isinglass that now appears in season on all the local chemists' counters in the cider country. Wine-making crops up in all fruit districts, especially where French or Flemish settlers have thirsted for home.

Where a valley is given over to orchards for fruit growing there is a considerable amount of work among the trees all the year round; they are lime washed (63), belly-banded against creeping moth, sprayed, pruned and tended assiduously, right through till harvest. We know of one fruit grower, returned from the States, who is trying out a new idea of combating late frosts with smudge fires. These are laid down the open tracks of the orchard, ready for instant lighting. Bees form a definite part of orchard work, though they are often kept by entirely separate individuals; they are needed for the fruit, and the sale of honey is considerable in all valley country.

The pollard willows and osier "hopes" along the lower water-courses are definitely connected with the fruit-growing industry, for there are made the hundreds and hundreds of baskets, pads, tuns, etc. (85) needed for the fruit and vegetable harvest. An osier hope is easily constructed on any convenient marsh land near the river by thrusting in the cut withy wands, which readily root. The stronger withies from the pollard willows are cut every five or seven years, and some hurdles are made, both for the sheep in the orchard and for protection of the soft fruits, and corn may be grown as the handiest way of getting straw for the strawberries.

Nowadays the east side of England is taking over the growing of fruit to a very great extent, but if you can get enough sun to ripen them, the wet West valleys will give you the juiciest strawberries and finest raspberries and currants, while there is still room for a considerable amount of soft fruit growing amid their orchards.

Up beyond Tewkesbury, which used to grow notable mustard, market gardening is very general; in fact, all round the valleys the growing of special crops is a speciality, governed by marketing possibilities as much as local conditions. Celery, brussels sprouts, spring onions (84), lettuces, all manner of green vegetable crops belong to the valley country. The bright scarlet alders of the Somerset marshes find their way up through Tewkesbury market for tying up long celery, and there are queer local industries, such as the netting of bags for brussels sprouts and pokes for new potatoes.

To the valleys the hill sheep are brought down for fattening, and the ewes for lambing in the spring; they crop in the grass orchards, and pigs thrive on the waste greens and roots of the market-gardening districts and serve to manure the land. They are kept for this purpose by some orchard owners. For the sheep and grazing animals kept for manuring the land there are some extra roots grown, but nothing like so many as on the arable plough lands. Grazing on river lands is always good, for it is astonishing how stock will fatten on dried-up grass, and apparently scant feeding, provided they have access to water, and certainly all beasts enjoy a river through their pastures. It may be something to do with the content engendered by a river! The valley cows stand about knee-deep in cool water, while the bees drone along the hedges, hayfields bleach in the sun, and all the river valley land holds peace . . . a peace and richness that belongs to the milking cow, for these lush green

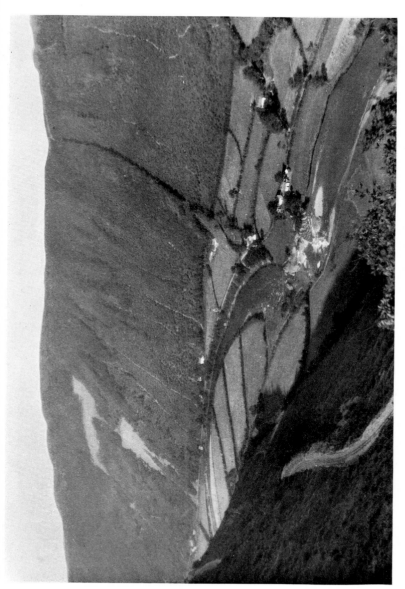

62   THE RHEIDOL VALLEY THREADING THE CARDIGANSHIRE HILLS

63 SPRAYING FRUIT-TREES WITH LIME

64 HURDLING IN HAMPSHIRE

river valleys are the milk bowls of England. We skim the cream from them in Devon, but the Vale of Pewsey, the Thames Valley, Aylesbury, all the river valleys with easy access to London, fill the town milk bottles, as the Dee valley, the valleys of the Yorkshire Ouse and rich grass lands of the North supply the Northern towns.

In the Severn valley the Gloucestershire district has long been famous for its cheese, which is interesting, as, with Cheshire, it is apparently a "lowland" district, and the higher lands are on the whole considered better for cheese, the wet longer grass being thought better for milk. However, Gloucester and the Dee valleys are both set in the cup of the hills, so perhaps the country theory holds. The cheese district of the Severn valley begins where the tilted orchards cease, and the wide, sloping hillsides are good for grazing and the meadows for hay and winter feed. Haymaking time in the lower Severn valley fills the air with that most wonderful country scent of new-mown hay, and the swaying, glossy fields are barely cleared before the corn crops are ready for carrying. The hay- and corn-stacks of the lower Severn valley are some of the best finished in England. The Trent valley may be as good, but the ricks run smaller, and stackyards are more common. A Gloucestershire haystack, perhaps done for one of the local stacking competitions, is a sheer constructional joy, and you will still find the gay barley-tailed birds and finely plaited straw ornaments on the handsome stacks of the West.

A good supply of hay was traditionally important at the widening of the Severn valley, for there the routes of the old cattle drovers led the black cattle from the West, and the red cattle from the North, down to the market, and it seems that probably some of the lower water meadows date from this time. These droves of hundreds of cattle were herded along the same definite routes every year. The cattle were in charge of special experienced drovers, and they had a very marked influence on arranging the country life and industries of the valleys into which they descended. At Clun, on the near side of the big border hills, is a very well-marked sorting depot, capable of accommodating enormous droves of cattle, and dealing with the drainage and manure question, the foddering and distribution. There are the marks of the old blacksmith's shop, for some of the cattle would be shod, if continuing to London. The skins and offal from the large slaughter houses of Bristol and Gloucester would produce their own industries. Incidentally, the neat's hair in the plasterwork of the buildings of this district is quite distinct from the more perishable "straw bound"

L

plaster or solid cob of the West. This neat's hair in the plaster always tracks a cattle or droving district, more than a milk-producing area. The by-products of the cattle districts produced the huge soap-boiling works of Bristol, which were famous for centuries. Working on logical conclusions alone, we unearthed the Llanthony horn works near Gloucester, a small part of what was once the great horn industry of the district, which for centuries made the horn utensils in everyday use. In earlier days, when more variety of organic manures was tried, the interior of the horns and all bones and offal, including dried blood, were preserved for fertilising; the bone-dust mills, glue-renderers and some bone products remain. Similarly the hides of the sheep from the hills above are worked where the water of the valley is suitable, and you find cowhide leather, sheepskin works and tanneries all along the old tracks of the drovers.

Beyond Gloucester is the end of our valley where the Severn sweeps round to the sea, and the bore of the sea sweeps up with the tide. Most of our largest rivers have this characteristic bore; the Trent has a large one and the small rivers by Grange and Ambleside also have their tidal wave. Here the Severn valley widens out into the low flat plains. To the south lie the level marsh lands of North and West Somerset, with their isolated island hills; the escarpment of the rocky ledge of Cheddar Gorge in the South, and small strange mounds, like Brent Knoll along the coast. Here, the orchard and garden countries end in level green fields, intercepted by the "rhines" or dykes (83)—very fine grazing country and rich water meadows. If you visit the orchard and valley country in the spring, then finish here; where these wide flat fields are fresh and green; while wet-winged ducks, with gold feet, splash in the dykes, making ridiculous noises, and, panicking in little drifts, are soft little yellow downy ducklings. Here, yellow and soft, sweep the dusty willow catkins across the streams. The wet, muddy roads are rutted silver with warm western rain. Come in cowslip time, when, below a white wind-swept sky, the silver world is caught under a net of yellow shaking cowslips, and beyond lies the wide silver estuary; while in the distance, little churches are tip-tilted among the shifting sand dunes, where the river valley reaches the sea.

Each river valley has its own character, and each differs one from the other; the solid Trent flowing between the undulating arable land; the Ouse, widening out of the Yorkshire plains before the long Humber estuary; the Thames river valley; the small, deep river valleys of Devon. So with the Vales,

65 CLEARING WOODS ABOVE THE WYE VALLEY

66 IN THE FOREST OF DEAN

67 LUMBER-WORK IN SOMERSET. Notice the Tethered Pulley

Aylesbury specialising in ducks, the Kent valleys full of hop gardens; each valley is diverse from the next, but the sequence of life and work down each of them holds fairly accurately.

The short Devon river valleys run their cider, fruit and cream all together in their short, swift courses. Devon cream and Cornish differ slightly; the method of all these clotted creams differs from that of plain cream as heat is used. The cream is "set-out" in wide panshons over gentle heat, and the clotted fluffy yellow-streaked cream is skimmed up in great gouts. The separator is sometimes used in Devon, but not to make Devonshire cream, and sometimes where a separator is used to obtain the cream for butter, the butter itself is still "come by" by the old Devon method of hand beating. They make many good cream cheeses in the West valleys, and the small orchards and gardens grow delicious fruit where there is room to do so.

In Kent valleys the round of the year belongs to the hop-growing specialists. The surrounding hill and down country used to supply the hop poles and standards from the high underwood, but now that wire is more generally used the demand is less. The old method of planting hops, four or five to a hill, lasts in name though the hop gardens are flat now, and rows have superseded groups. With the old group system the bines tended to form a dense bunch high overhead, blocking out sun and air. The present wire training produces finer hops, and is everywhere general. Early in the spring, local labour, very generally women folk, spend hours in the fields training the young shoots gently round the string to ensure even distribution. It is one of the pleasantest jobs, judging by the chat and laughter that goes on in the spring sunshine, and some of the hands who have been teaching Robin Hop the way he should go, so tenderly, for years, are remarkably quick and skilful on the job. The strings overhead are put up by the men on stilts, seven or eight feet high (68, 69), spidering about. Hoeing and clearing between the rows continue all summer (and Tull would have delighted in some of the contraptions). The Kentish plough is sometimes used there, and sometimes in the cherry orchards. At harvest time the Kent hopyards gain by being close to accessible labour from the East End of London. For a few weeks East London moves into the country and dwells in settlements, camps and caravans in the same villages of Kent. I studied once in a large oast house, where the requests for hop bins were coming in as early as June. Hundreds of letters were filed for reference. The boss knew most of them and reserved their bins as a matter of course, and sometimes five or six bins were now required by a family which had originally been one unit, but which had spread yearly, bringing extra babies and sisters, cousins and aunts, till an entire district pervaded one corner of the hop garden. A good many requests were from families wanting to give their children a holiday in the fresh air, for the sleepy, hot, hop-picking holiday is thought the finest thing in the world for children.

The newest drying of the hops by hot air from coal, coke and anthracite fires has slowed up the charcoal burners' job on the downs, and the larch pole and wire has brought down the value of the surrounding downside underwood, though enormous piles of brushwood and faggots pile up beside the new high imported hop poles.

Kent cherry orchards are another example of a specialised industry which has a few intensive weeks of harvesting to end a year of intermittent attention. As in our other river and orchard districts, the side industries of willow basket making, slat-cutting, barrel and hoop making in the surrounding woods, "join on" to the fruit-growing industry in the valley itself. Kent cherry orchards are grassy as a whole, and but few of them are organised with the commercial intensity of the newer East Anglian fruit farms. As soon as the fruit ripens, bird scarers live in each orchard, and the popping of their guns punctuates the day from early dawn onwards. Mostly "bird men" live out all day in the orchard, with their neat little fire and boiling kettle in front of their little hut shelter. The cherries are gathered into locally made baskets, and each basket is supplied with an iron hook for hitching it on to the branches. The ladders are also a local speciality, being very wide, up to three feet wide at the base and tapering to a foot or nine inches at the top according to their length. These characteristic splay foot affairs seem to be found nowhere else in England; like many things in Kent, they are a unique local production. Thousands of miles away, in a citrus estate in Rhodesia, two men were discussing the orange-picking apparatus required by their native boys. They argued one way, and explained another, and got nothing fixed, till one man volunteered to "teach them to make cherry ladders!" Then they were all able to go and get a drink in peace. I mention this to show how these small individualisms make bonds between us all!

Cherries that are gathered during the day are taken up to London overnight in great lorries, and arrive in time for Covent Garden market in the early dawn. Locally, the fruit is made into pies, jams and bottled, but there's no great attempt at preserving or tinning, and cherry ale and cherry brandy are

68, 69 WORK IN THE HOP-FIELDS

72　THE CARTWRIGHT

73　INSIDE THE OAST-HOUSE

made of the sour dark Morello cherries that grow well in the Trent valleys. Sometimes a certain district in a warm sheltered valley has a sudden phenomenal crop of mushrooms; sometimes a valley will specialise in pigs or poultry in its orchards.

There are innumerable industries to mark the individuality of all valleys. Ducks and geese belong specially to river valleys, with their correlated industry of feather dressing and cleansing, while bolster and pillow-making is usually to be found, with water-power corn mills for the locally grown poultry feed. Though Orpington hens have a name for themselves, like Aylesbury ducks, the large hen farms are mostly in the undulating Midlands.

The professional rat catcher is usually a valley-born man, because in the confined area of the valleys outbreaks of rats, or vermin of any sort, spread much more rapidly and intensively than elsewhere. Also, please notice that when you come down from the mountain-tops to the wooded valleys, the bar parlours are strewed with sawdust, instead of being sanded.

CHAPTER V

FLATS AND FENS

" 'The olde sea wall (he cried) is downe,
   The rising tide comes on apace,
And boats adrift in yonder towne
   Go sailing uppe the market-place.'
He shook as one that looks on death:
'God save you, mother!' straight he saith;
'Where is my wife, Elizabeth?'

·   ·   ·

"Upon the roofe we sate that night,
   The noise of bells went sweeping by:
I marked the lofty beacon light
   Stream from the church tower, red and high—
A lurid mark and dread to see;
And awesome bells they were to mee,
That in the dark rang 'Enderby.' "

JEAN INGELOW, *High Tide on the Coast of Lincolnshire*

THERE is a fair amount of flat and fen land in England for its size. Generally speaking, there are three varieties of flat—the alluvial deposits, which is where rain and river have washed the land out to sea; salt marsh, where the sea has washed away from the land; and compromises between the two. The first is usually very fertile and the second usually very salt, but this generalisation is only a very rough division; practically every small flat district or fen and marsh in this island has been accounted for in each case in some slightly different way. Inland we have a few genuinely flat areas. Otmoor is a curious isolated little bit of fenland in Oxfordshire. Somerset of the marshes is genuinely flat, the small hills, church topped, being once islands left above the drowned land, and beyond Castle Cary the marsh district is abolutely distinct, genuine flat marsh, with square fields, deep dykes, called locally "rhines" (83), and long plantings of osiers by the embankments. The whole air over this district is genuine marsh flat, with the wheeling birds crying out in the open sky, the gurgle of water and the lush green of wet land. Hereabouts plaited basket work of all kinds is done, and there are standing sheds by the long dykes where the wands stand to season, and loads wrapped into great round faggots are sent along the Great

74 BROXBOURNE MILL ON THE LEA, HERTFORDSHIRE

75 INTENSIVE MARKET-GARDENING NEAR LONDON : Glass-houses at Cheshunt

West Road. Farther up, towards Hungerford there is the Kennet with its flat floor, where definitely the marsh is of the river valley type, of running water, flowering reeds and rushes and all the change that comes with flowing river water. In the West there are some water meadows by the sea below the Severn, and the long neck out to Newnham Ferry in Gloucestershire, which is genuine flat land. The canal and embankment bound it on the river side, and the fields stretch flat back to the Cotswolds. Near the marsh grazing on these level fields is the stronghold of the old Gloucester cheesemakers. Slimbridge and district still makes the genuine old farmhouse Gloucester cheese, "trundles," "double Gloucester," all traditional, a rich and very good cheese. The plain of Cheshire has a somewhat similar cheese, but the Cheshire plain is drier, the grass has not the lush quality and the cheese in general output is harder. The Cheshire cheese that comes up to London is usually a circular ginger-coloured brick, but where the Cheshire plain peters out against the line of the Welsh Hills you can still get the old soft crumbly Cheshire cheese, which is pale cream.

The Wirral peninsula is flat—very, very flat: the bright pink houses and green trees stand on it like toys set up on a tray, and towards the end, where the sea wind blows in, are all tilted at one angle, as if someone had jogged God's elbow. The end peters out into Port Sunlight and Birkenhead overflow, but within a mile of the high road in any direction lie quiet farmlands, and there are good horses about.

The sands of Dee are really sands, across which the ill-fated Mary went to call the cattle home, and when "the rolling tide is cold and dank with foam" they are about as mournful as the song. On the east the Ouse opens out into the estuary of the Humber between salt marshes and alluvial deposit in the warpings.

Now the district around here shows a treatment you find nowhere else in England on the same scale. The huge level peaty sea marshes were practically useless, but the surface peat-moss has been made into an industry for peat-litter packing; the stuff was teased up and milled and some of it was exported as far as Nigeria, as peat-moss litter. The residue was used to mop up the oil and molasses in the making of cowcake. Where the peat-moss has gone is a pretty level track. After the initial expense of cutting an irrigation canal, warping begins. A dyke lets the muddy foul estuary water rush in over the flats at high tide, all through the turn of the tide it stands stagnant, dropping its silt, till the water drains gently off at low water, leaving the mud behind. It is a perfectly natural process

that is actually going on between tides in almost every river
estuary, but here it is scientifically hurried up till they reckon
an average of three feet of good earth can be laid down in about
four years. After a consolidating sowing and some suitable
tillage, you have fields of extremely useful top tilth over a
fairly adequate peaty subsoil. Sometimes the warping has to be
repeated, and it is pretty necessary to change the direction of
the flow in the irrigation canal so as to get an even distribution
of mud, but on the whole it's a very interesting piece of
developing England.

South, in Lincolnshire are the historic flats of "high-tide on
the coast of Lincolnshire." The great dykes of the Dutchmen
held back the sea except at high tide, when of old, great bores
or waves broke through, and rushing up the river channel
swamped all the land. A watch was kept on the church towers
at all spring tides, and at the first danger the church bells were
rung, *pealing them upwards* in a horrible unaccustomed sound
that carried across the rising water like wild cries. At the danger
signal, herds and flocks must be driven inland, but even so life
was claimed by the sea for years. Nowadays the land lies level
and calm under the sea haze of hot summer, and in the winter
the sheep and the milking pastures are drained by square dykes.
Inland, clamps and clamps of potatoes stretch alongside the
straight dykes, and dotted about the flat green fields are the
characteristic little high cottages of old red brick, or tarred
brick and timber, very small, very square and sometimes three
stories high with a chimney at the top corner looking as if it
was craning its neck to see its neighbour miles and miles away
across the level.

Southwards across the Wash, either side of Wells in Norfolk,
are some few sea marshes. To the west there is a bird island,
where you can be taken over and spend the night, and, if you are
lucky, watch migrations hopeful, and arrivals tired, and spend
happy hours during the nesting seasons. Eastwards, the long
embankment of the old sea wall holds out in a far ridge to the
north, and drowned green meadows and muddy inlets lie two
miles wide between it and the shore. Well I know that embankment; years ago I walked around that long low coast from the
cliffs of Cromer. It was a cold wet February day, and sticking
close and wet foot along the shore I kept on and on, till in the
dusk I was upon the old sea wall; far beyond deserted and
winter-shuttered Sheringham. Winter evening in February and
rain falling. I think it was one of the most lonesome walks I
have ever followed. Night fell, and the sea moaned at my side,
a gull screamed out like a lost soul over the misty marshes.

76 WATERCRESS BEDS IN HERTFORDSHIRE

77 CARTING MANGOLDS IN KENT

78 THE OLD QUAY AND WINDMILL, Cley-next-the-Sea, Norfolk

The tide was coming in, there was a line of white spray on the right, and on my left, dimly lit, I could see swampy green dykes, and hear the slopping of water in rough sodden grass. Behind me I had passed a low break in the wall, where by now the rising water must be washing over. Onwards, therefore, in hope of finding a way across the marshes leading inland. Who says England is overcrowded? Not a soul all that day did I see. In the dark, mocking me across the wide morass, came occasionally the shine from some cottage window, the yellow light wagging to me across the water, but between us lay a flooded morass of impenetrable mud cut by dykes that gurgled in black unknown depths. I tell you, it was lonesome along that barren sea wall. By daylight, one could have located some possible track across the marshes, but now in the dark there was nothing to do but plod helplessly along, only the sea moaning on my right, and the flood sobbing on my left. . . .

Then the wall ended . . . groping in the wet dark I could feel the broken cement blocks peter out in sand, drift shingle and mud; and around the dead-end swirled dark water sucking at me. A most unpleasant spot! A wave broke on my right, and the salt spray fell dropping showers over me. It didn't make much difference I'd reached the wet end of the lost world. I crawled round on the lee side on to the cold wet cement slabs, grovelled a hole in the mud and got into it out of the wind. The mud closed around me as I sat, all night long. Whaups cried hopelessly, and the wind and the sea moaned and howled. All night long the water sucked and sobbed around me, and mud and I were one. As the dawn came, damp and grey over the mud, there moved a misty wet ghost with a limp string bag—as the dim shade quelched slowly past I rose stiffly: "Ho!" I called, speaking as one corpse to another, "Where am I?"—"Clay" (Cley) it said (I felt it).—"Where are you going?"—The echo came mournfully over the marsh. "I'm going after wour-r-rms." I staggered toward him, and he gathered me in.

A white mist covered the sea, a grey mist covered the land, I lugged my shoes out of their mud sockets, and hung them round my neck, and plodded waist-deep, his waders gulping before me. I do not know when I felt worse! But later I had the sort of breakfast that begins with rum, and ends with fried cockles and bacon and jam, and felt much better, because it was the sort of breakfast for which you wear landlady's alpaca gown over her son's old flannel breeches, two blankets (à la Julius Caesar), and carpet slippers tied on with string. . . .

M

Somehow, whenever one tries to write *Magnificat* about English country people, it always becomes a *Nunc Dimittis*! they are so splendidly kind. I learnt about the worms later; They really are a regular job of work and industry of the flats. You get the best sorts where mud and sea sand mingle. They are collected, gutted, with one unpleasant movement of the thumb, and delivered in bags and kegs for bait. I believe they keep quite well; they have to be guarded from rats. The white worm is got farther inland; he looks whitish and succulent, like banana spawn. The price is not excessive, for there is usually a steady demand, and an expert wormer of good repute has a reliable clientèle, and is a very important link between the devil and the deep sea. (I believe we have mentioned elsewhere that the pith of the marsh reed makes bodies for some fishing flies.)

Most flats of Suffolk and Essex are the drowned river valley type. South of Ipswich along the Stour estuary is a small typical strip which I had reason to study very closely, as it was the marsh farmland of Tusser's *Hundred Points of Good Husbandry*, and in spite of the new railway cutting which has entirely altered the aspect of the estuary (bringing up overwhelming quantities of the subsoil), and the new buildings south of Holbrook, much of the old marsh wall and many of the salt grazings can be tracked out under the sixteenth-century map. As the mountain mutton was served with thyme and green herbs, so the marsh mutton from the salt grazings was served with laver and samphire, and sea greens (*vide* "Seacoast and Estuaries," p. 109). Eels almost count as an inland industry, but had better be discussed in the same place. Mersey Island, Maldon, Pinmill, Burnham and all the flat lands of this district and the Thames estuary seem to belong to the yachtsman and the little shipowners. Flat land and marshes line the Thames estuary as far as Whitstable.

An utterly different type of flat is farther south in Romney Marsh, which are marshes in name only; they are firm grazing and arable fields (79), their character as marsh land (originally of alluvial deposit) being only in their absolutely level surface, and the straight-set dyke drains. Romney Marsh is a true level of England. There are very few farms; the pasturage is looked after by shepherds, called "lookers," whose sheep-walks may cover as much as three hundred acres of smooth level thick green grass. In the summer the seaside population now brings many visitors to this part of the South coast, and the long high roads across the marshes are whitened with the dust of passing cars.

79 SHEEP ON ROMNEY MARSH: The grazing is rich, but the life is hard

80 THE ROAD ACROSS SEDGEMOOR, SOMERSET, seen from the Polden Hills

81   NEW POTATOES FOR THE LONDON MARKET:
Opening up a Clamp near Maidstone, Kent

82   PLANTING POTATOES IN KENT

Where there is a local sale of milk in summer there are a few cows, but on the whole it is sheep, not cattle, pasturage. The marsh itself is very quiet; the level, almost stagnant ditches are deep with bullrushes and flowering rush, and the raised dykes and trackways shelter thin wind-torn hedges; the purple sloe grows thickly there, and all the land is within sound of the sea. It is very thinly populated, and even in times when some of the land was arable it had a name for fevers and rheumatism, and was unpopular for everything but its wonderful grazing. Hereabouts are some of the most extraordinary grazing fields in England. They are treated with something of the reverence that is given to the precious green lawns of ancient colleges, and some of them have not been broken within a hundred years. The old folk on the marshes consider that these fields are the only ones worthy to rank as real grazing, maintaining "that marsh land once broken is never again any use." Some of these fields have been tended and treated with seeds of various grasses, but the grazing itself is the real cultivation of the marsh pastures, even as "close cutting" is the cultivation of the fine lawn. None of the rich grazing land there is ever allowed to stand for hay, as it would spoil the close quality of the bite. As soon as the grass begins to come up, the sheep are herded on to the land, practically shoulder to shoulder, and eat off this first growth; they call this *tegging*. Later, the sheep are herded into their separate fields in more reasonable numbers, and the special pasture fields, with their almost incredible richness of bite, are reserved for fattening off the sheep as they come forward! Some of these rich fields will take fifty sheep to the acre, and it has been known, when a flock was late in returning from the downs, to hold a hundred to the acre for "first bite." The Romney Marsh sheep themselves are a very individual breed. They are said to be of Flemish origin, and certainly they have an Anne of Cleves look! Long bodied, short strong thick-boned legs, white face, with large noses, broad head—a very good brain has your Romney marsh sheep!—thick-set neck and wool growing low down on their foreheads. Their noses should be shaded dark, and their fleece more thick and strong than soft. In character they are more like the mountain sheep, being good foragers, with an ability to think for themselves. To crouch down out of the icy sea wind on the lee side of a shuddering wind-torn thorn bush, and watch the marsh sheep grazing on a long chilly afternoon is to realise why they, too, have braved the narrow seas and travelled abroad! If you watch, they crop in a business-like way, not following each other, but each one attending strictly to his own business. An old ewe will throw up her head, look round and then stump off determinedly to hunt up a special juicy patch that she "knows to," or some others will energetically scrape away a small sprinkling of snow with their feet. They have good reason to be hardy, these raw-boned sheep of Romney Marsh. The lambs come in April, and when wool was a better price were sometimes sheared the first year! Unfortunately they are very large, and now "small lamb" is fashionable. The whole marsh resounds, about August, with cries, while the lambs are being sorted out and sent up on to the downs. They don't fatten on the downs, but it keeps them going, and as a shepherd explained "on that sparse grazing, they learn to keep their eyes open, and get busy, so that they fatten all the sooner when they return to the marsh in the following spring." Like the mountain sheep, their shepherd "lookers" reckon they "don't do well on turnips." If they give them turnip "the marsh is no good to them afterwards *and there you are!*" "Exactly," you agree, sheltering behind a three-foot embankment, while an Arctic upchannel blast pierces through your coat. "Baa!" says a Romney Marsh ewe, her white fleece standing up like a Flemish bonnet around her strong-nosed intelligent face! The Romney sheep are a breed exported for crossing abroad. They are good bone and hardy training makes them worthy colonists!

Romney Marsh adjoins the flat land of Dungeness. Here the level is completely different, being of shingle, gradually piled up by the washing seas. A curious bit of land; at the far end it stands out into deep water, clashing down into the five-fathom line about a hundred yards from shore. Within the last two years this stretch of shingle has been very rapidly built over, and already a road made of wood, wire netting and cement is travelling out to the far end. Before then the only roads were the little tracks between the fisher huts, made by trailing tar over the shingle and treading in sand, so that a rambling trackway led like a sticky trickle of toffee over the crumbly shingle. On the east a green rim of grass joins on to Romney Marsh and Walland Marsh, but beyond lie level acres of this grey, sea-cleansed shingle, wide and flat, and laced over with lines of driftwood, and trailing tiny flowers and weeds. There are plantations of low holly and gorse bushes sheared by the wind. Sea-borne clouds blow in across the sky and trail blue shadows over the stony world. Inland in the smoke-scented evening the young moon hangs low in a mist over the downs, and on the west is a bird sanctuary. The terns have a colony here, and when the eggs are out, one must walk wet foot between the tides of the shore, for the terns with their shining black heads, slender wings and tiny scarlet feet, tilt up and down with troubled anxious cries, over eggs invisible to us, lying among the shingle. It was here I once saw an avocat. The growth of the earth upon this shingle land is demonstrated around any of the small households, which have long made weatherboarded and black-tarred resistance to

stone and sea. Household rubbish that within a year becomes beaten to pulp by the pounding shingle is then the basis for tiny gardens, three and four feet wide, gardens literally scratched out of the shingle, and fed with burnt seaweed, scraps of burnt cloth, dead leaves and every single scrap of organic matter that can be

THE SHINGLE-DWELLER'S
WHEELBARROW

induced to lodge between the crevices of the stones. They haven't the depth for root crops yet, but I've had a lettuce off the shingle, and one enterprising agriculturalist *thought he "might go to a radish at the deep end!"* Below the hollows of the shingle, there's plenty of clear water; you've only to dig down a few feet in some places to find it gurgling wet. Goats are kept

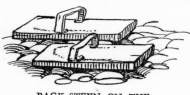

BACK-STEYN ON THE
SHINGLE

on the thin green-netted shingle, and there are quantities of hare, whose runways mark out long silver tracks that show up in some lighting like the pattern on watered silk,

The purple branching sea-kale grows well in places, heavenly blue, and crisp as celery. Where shingle and earth meet are drifts of foxgloves, which used to be harvested for the chemist's digitalis. An unexpected item to find in this shingle land is the honey. After miles of level stony shingle it is almost incredible to find an active hive of prize-winning honey bees, down near the coastguards; however, the close flowers of the shingle, though small, are incredibly fragrant; the yellow broom and a few wild flowers in that windy land have a scent of quite exceptional strength, especially on a hot day when the air is blowing in from the sea, and these almost invisibly close-growing flowers among the shingle perhaps serve to give the honey its distinct "hymetus" flavour.

These levels are the land of the back-steyn. The shingle is so impossible to walk on that the natives have made slats of wood, about eighteen inches long and ten inches wide, with a loop of leather which they slip over their boots and use in the method of the "duckboards" of the marsh, only, being dry, you can rattle over the shingle at a better rate than you can scoop (like reluctant butter) over the mud. It is rather amusing to a visitor to see the coastguard rattle down to post on two wooden boards, and the curate rattle up to the Sunday School on a pair of wooden boards, and the maiden in the gloaming rattling off

A CART FOR USE ON SHINGLE OR SAND

to meet her lover on a pair of wooden boards, but at the end of the week you get so used to going about on a pair of wooden boards yourself that you don't notice it! Now they've built a new road the back-steyn will soon be relegated to beach and bathers, but the fishermen will still need them, and over this flat land will still trundle their great barrel-wheeled carts, with flanges three feet wide—the only vehicles which would roll over a shingle beach to bring the fish up off the boats.

Pevensey levels have the "valley" characteristics almost more than true "levels," but Selsey Bill lies at the end of a most individual tract of level country. There used to be harbour and quay behind Pagham, for the farmers of "the Bill." This has now become a broken-sided millrace. The fields around are some arable and a few pasturage, but last year when I was there wide stretches were yellow with turnip, and great quantities of Southdowns were being fattened up for market. Along this level they've got the most curious traditional field method of "leading" which you will find nowhere else in

83 A SOMERSET "RHINE" OR DRAIN ON QUEENSMOOR

84 WASHING WHITE CRISP SPRING ONIONS IN THE VALE
OF PERSHORE

85 BASKET-WORK IN GLOUCESTERSHIRE

England. Rolling, harrowing, etc., all manner of "field leading"
is done at the end of a ten-feet long pole, the man walking
level with the horse's head, sideways ten feet distant. It is the
queerest-looking way of doing things you ever
did see! "Does everyone do it in these parts?"—
"Yes."—"Do you do it when you go to other
parts?"—"*We* don't go to other parts!"—
"Oh!"—"That chap, he came from other parts;
but he does it this way, now he's come to these
parts." If you watch perhaps two ploughs, a
harrow and a roller, all working simultaneously,
passing straight up, passing straight down, to
and fro over one large level field, on a blowing
driving day, when dun-coloured ash pole is invisible against dun-coloured earth, you can see
only eight sets of men and horses, all sliding
up and down past each other at equal distances.
It is a queer fashion, but there seems no need
to change it! The poles are attached to the "bit
piece" (as in a bull pole), the feering is very
straight, the horses plod along very steadily:
"*we do it this way in these parts.*" There's a very
good working windmill on Selsey Bill. In the
summer the owner makes a side line by showing
it to visitors at sixpence a head.

On most marshes and levels eels are caught
by the usual eel traps and nettings, and by
several extremely unusual and interesting local
methods. Sniggling is almost a poaching trick,
a straightened fish-hook, slender nail, or very
strong pack needle is driven into a long stake
and baited with a worm; the fisher then walks
by the banks where the eels are, their heads just
sticking up through the mud, and slithers the
worm-adorned stick down to the notice of a
good-sized eel; as the head moves preparatory
to engulfing the bait, a second stick is brought
down with a whack upon the back of the head,
impaling the gullet on the hook, and held
between the two sticks the eel is then with-

AN EEL SPEAR

drawn from the mud. Much more hefty are the eel spears
of the deep dykes. These are great heavy ash poles, ten,
fourteen, or twenty feet long, to the ends of which the
splayed eel hooks of steel fourteen inches long fan out like
a fish tail. The weight of a strong eel spear is sufficient

to carry it driving downwards through the mud several feet, yet the strong-armed broad-shouldered dyke men will swing them overhead in a steady dripping wheel, letting them go with a running splash as they slide through their strong hands and spear down into the dark dyke. The fish-tail splaying of the steel hook spreads it in the mud, and the withdrawing, hauling action closes it with a grip upon the dark wriggling eel. The first time I watched this eel-spearing was in the evening. The reeds of the dyke had been weaving to me stories of "Mare Swallow" (Hereward the Wake's horse), and the Saxons were standing, broadswords and quarter-staff swinging, through the strongholds of the fens. . . . Suddenly! before me, in the dusk, raised high on the dyke silhouetted against the sky, stood an all-square sturdy Saxon, bare armed and rough of hair, with loose trousers tied in at knee and ankle where his feet were thrust into stout rough leather shoes. High in a wide swinging circle round his broad shoulders, swung a defence of ten feet stout ash wood, barbed with iron, a Saxon quarter-staff. The water-drops wheeled and swung from it while he spun it with a steady strong swing in the "guard" and "defence" movements, that I had seen last in an early English manuscript. The figure walked quietly along the dyke whirling the staff, head bent, looking down into the water below. He walked over fifty yards of fen; through the gathering dusk of English evening, from the eleventh century into the twentieth. . . . He was an eel-spearer. . . .

THE FENS

To understand the fens it is necessary to have an outline idea of how they were formed. Originally a chalk barrier from Hunstanton to Skegness stretched across the Wash. The Ice Age intervened, and after setting a few geological jigsaw puzzles all across Norfolk, left a sort of tidal pool, in which the bones of hippopotamus and rhino got left behind. In the natural course of an incredibly long time, the inland water, washing down through the tidal pool into the new North Sea, washed out most of the old boulder clay, and filled the space up with land mud. Beyond, at the meeting of the outgoing water with the incoming tide, there heaped up sand dunes, and over all a stagnant morass of peat formed. The whole formation was as erratic and irregular as the mess you will find in any shallow mud puddle which drains into rising and falling water. Centuries-old tree stumps are found far below low-water mark, and shells far above high-water mark. These are the fens that

86 A FENLAND RIVER : The Ouse at Wiggenhall St. Germans, Norfolk

87   HAND-HOEING SUGAR-BEET IN ESSEX

88   DRAWING HAY IN A SCOW ON THE NORFOLK BROADS

the Romans started draining. Reports vary, but we know there was a great inundation (probably the worst) about 1236, and through the medieval mixture of truth and mystery, we hear that the war of the fens continued. In Charles I's time Sir Cornelius Vermuyden was asked to undertake the work of draining the fens, but the Civil War hung up the project. Then Francis, Earl of Bedford, and thirteen other gentlemen tackled it as a private "Adventure," but the trouble between fresh water and sea water was as nothing to the trouble between the landowners and the adventurers, and (like peat), the government settled between the two. Finally, in 1653 the son of the original Earl of Bedford and a fresh company working with Vermuyden on his original plan pulled it off, and the two great cuts called the "Bedford Rivers" commemorate their achievement.

Of old, the fens had many specialities unknown to the rest of England. Kingsley's *Hereward the Wake*, inaccurate as it may be historically, gives a very good description of the actual life in those wild inaccessible small island strongholds. Queer paths were made by cutting bundles and faggots of reed, long poles were used for a running jump to carry across the net-like water courses. The pole leap of our sports to-day is upright, the pole being used to lift, and give height, and being dropped as the athlete clears the bar, but in those days the old pole leap was to carry across the dyke, and you did not release the pole, but carried it with you. All manner of small craft were built to thread their way along the narrow waterways, and at a period when plenty of fresh meat and game (none of your salted old dried hogmeat for the fenmen!) and an unlimited supply of fish were available, the fen country did not have such a bad aspect. In later years, when agriculture was God, the landed gentry thought it was the most God-forsaken place on earth. To get the right perspective of the fens, you must hear the reeds waving in the wind, the ceaseless lapping of water, the cry of wild-fowl, smell peat and the savour of roasting wild birds on the wild moorlike uplands—and realise the great quantities of heavy stone they thought it worth while to import at such trouble and expense to build the great abbeys. Nothing speaks so eloquently of the change in the fens as one small old bridge at Croyland. It is a steep, incredibly strong heavy stone-built triangular bridge. Its steep sides, almost stairway steep, must, even when the stones were laid with turf and stranded reed, have been a stiff climb for a laden donkey or weary man. The stone copings are worn smooth with generations of resting travellers and loafers and *the stone breastway*

N

below is water worn where the reeds of three rivers passed below. Now the bridge feels no water but the falling rain, and few footsteps but those of the children endlessly playing up and down, and down and up, and along the dusty wide white high street of Croyland the motor cars sweep past to Croyland Abbey. Should I send strangers to the Fens for the first time, I do not think I should send them straight to Ely, wonderful as Ely is, but to Croyland, and I think they should go across from North to East in September, when the heather of Norfolk uplands is bronze and the bracken gold, and they shall sweep across the fields which are bleaching to the winter frosts, and pass high along straight dykes, where the withering reeds whistle and rustle. They shall see, from rough rising ground, acres and acres of parti-coloured fenland, bronze-green, purple-white, scratched with silver, where the white sky shines on the dykes below. Towards evening, beyond rich brown-wet ploughed land and long potato clamps, they shall come to green pasture fields, and sheep and cattle moving quietly over a dyke bridge to their farm to be milked, and at nightfall they shall reach Croyland Abbey. Then the turn of the incoming tide shall bring dark rain, and the wind shall rise and scream through the torn thorn trees, and crash and thrash in the hollow high reeds, and send the water creaming and hissing through the tussocky grass to the edge of the dyke. Then in the windswept dark when the tide is up and the Wash is full of water, they shall hear the sound of Croyland Abbey bells, pealing out over broken resounding water; one of the most beautiful sounds in England.

More than any other part of England the character of the fens is interlocked with the character of the fenland people. They have always been a strange sturdy independent race. Historically they have the name for being "intolerant of rule, and fiercely rebellious." Their life, their work and their sport were always distinct from the other parts of Britain. There's a strong Dutch-like element among them, as there is along much of our East lowland coast. Both for the dykes and the weaving, Chaucer's Merchant desired to keep safe the Eastern seaboard.

One sport that particularly belongs to the fens is skating. In our island climate frost very seldom stays for long, but if it holds anywhere it is in the fens and the East, where the long straight waterways and the wide broads make a paradise for skaters, and where at the first ring of the frost all the district is out flying along the ice in the cold clear air of East England.

The reeds and peat are the two characteristic fenland products. Withies and basketry the fens share with every river

89 BULB CULTURE IN THE FENS : A Narcissus Field near Spalding

90 A WINDING BROADLAND RIVER : The Ant, near Stalham, Norfolk

91 A SLUGGISH FENLAND RIVER : Low Tide on the Witham at Boston

valley in England (though the basketry of the country varies tremendously, and I've counted a dozen different kinds). One form of basketry which is a speciality of the fens is made from the shredded leaves of the reed. The reed itself, strong, straight and brittle, is not basketry material, but these pliant grey-green leaves and the long supple sedge leaves are variously used, plaited or wrapped. Some of the heavy baskets have the soft coiled quality of the shapes made of rope by the fisherfolk, and the fisherfolk are some of the best makers of these soft baskets. They are the fenland equivalent of the straw basketry of the Midland plains and the cornlands. Like the beehive basketry, its wrapped and folded texture gives it insulating qualities, which makes it very warm and utterly different from the plaited wickerwork.

A FEN BASKET (ALSO MADE IN DORSET)

The reeds are our very best English thatching material (94). Norfolk reed and Kent reed are slightly different, and a peculiar strong straw grown towards Wiltshire way used to be called reed. The fenland reed is of great length and strength, and a sound thatch of Norfolk reed will stand upwards of fifty years. The reeds are cut variously, usually with a wide long scythe, and great barges of the reed are floated down the rivers and lodes. The reeds have to be stacked until the folded leaves drop off them. "We stack till they drophan," as a thatcher told me. The reeds take their period of seasoning and are then bundled ready for the thatcher. There are two types of thatching; for churches and heavy stone buildings the gable ends come above the thickness of the thatch, and the thatch itself has a smooth close finish, which with the passing of time takes on a gloss, almost an iridescence, like the back of a very old dark pigeon, and is the most perfect architectural accompaniment for the flint building. For cottages and lower buildings the thatch overhangs the gables and the wall, in character slightly more similar to the heavy straw thatch of Devon (95). To get a good slope for thatch the pitch of the roof must be fairly steep so that the slanting reeds sloping out from the angle of incline may lie sufficiently above each other for the weight to pack them close, and yet have sufficient downward slope to shoot off the water.

Preparing to use reed thatch, strong stakes are laid across between the groynes, and the spacing at either end near the gable has to be so arranged that the packing width of the reed may not fall too heavily on this most thickly packed spot. The thatching is laid on from the eaves upwards, in wide strips, the comfortable width of the thatcher's reach, to the right hand as he faces the roof from his ladder (94). The tools are very simple; there is the graip, of various patterns, with which he carries up the reed, the stake, or hold, which rests it in position on the roof top, the bat, a sloping ended mallet of heavy wood, with which he beats the ends of the reed back into the sloping form

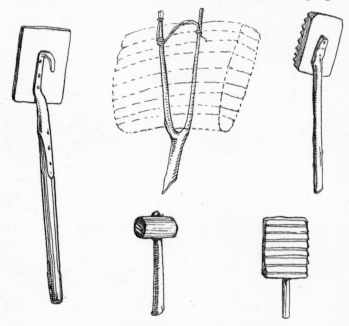

THE THATCHER'S TOOLS

of the finished roof. This sloping must not be got by too much beating; if you watch an expert you will see he gets it more by the sloping swing as he settles the bundle of reed in its place.

The reeds are secured variously, accordingly as the taste and experience of the thatcher decides, or the condition of the roof makes most suitable. The old osier-pegging with bent slits or double twisted prongs of willow seems superseded by sewing methods in a great many cases. A very good thatcher that I know uses now the heavy tarred twine of the fisherman for most of the work, and the wooden prong work only where extra depth and subsequent weight and strength of the under-pinning of the roof makes this practical.

The three- or four-feet iron needle carrying the tie is thrust

92   MENDING THE THATCH OF AN OLD COTTAGE NEAR WAREHAM, DORSET

93 MAKING BEE-SKIPS OF GOLD STRAW NEAR SIDMOUTH, DEVON

94 THATCHING WITH KENTISH REEDS

95   THATCHING A COB WALL IN OXFORDSHIRE

96   THE SPLIT STONE-SLATES OF THE COTSWOLDS

97 HOUGHTON MILL ON THE OUSE, HUNTINGDONSHIRE.
The interior is shown on Fig. 98

through the thatch, brought round the tie below and fastened above. A bent slat is then inserted under the groyne, sprung over the reed and inserted under the groyne at the far side, forming a spring which will automatically loosen and tighten with the light dryness or heavy wetness of the thatch.

Tusser's remark, "Where houses be reeded as houses have need, now pare off the moss, and go beating the reed," refers to the raising of the thatch, particularly a new thatch under its first onslaught of the weather. Hard frost particularly, just as it loosens the ground, will loosen the wet porous reed, and a thatch may be preserved intact much longer if, after the wet and frost of winter, the thatcher's wooden mallet be used with an upward motion against the ends of the reed, driving them up and in, and wedging the bundles tightly again under their spring-hold. A modern idea in thatching is a development of an old trick. In the fens, near waterways or the sea, the old fish-nets, too rotten or torn to be water-worthy, used to be thrown up over the thatching and pegged in. They served to prevent wind and frost breaking the thatch, and a little also to deter the birds from burrowing and nesting in it. The corn bunting was a terror for breaking through the thatching on corn-stacks, especially in hard weather; they would persevere

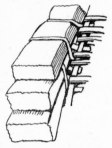

PINNING THATCH

until they got through and could haul out the ears of corn, and once they had found the way, other birds were quick enough to follow it up. Nowadays, many an old thatch hangs on under a covering of wire netting, and in one or two cases, with small cottages, I've known the second coat of thatch to be sewn on through the netting. It sounds incredible, but it worked. In exposed parts, a neat line of cement, or worked brick earth, is laid along the ridge pole and around the joins of the thatch; the house leek is sometimes planted purposely on a thatch. I've seen an Irish thatch which had a regular pattern of house leek planted in criss-cross rows, with pleasant effect.

Reed was also used to form trackways, great bundles cut and thrown down in the morass made possible temporary crossings. Bundles of reed were used for heating the brick baking-oven for bread. In an enclosed space, with a regulated draught, they gave out tremendous quick heat, though they were not really good for burning on the open hearth, where peat was more suitable fuel. The fenland peat is quite different in consistency from the moorland peat; the moorland has a basis of sphagnum moss, and the fenland has botanically somewhat different constituents. Hence there are two different varieties of peat fuel, the hard dark, solid sort, which dries slowly and burns with an intense slow heat, and the light almost fluffy kind which dries more quickly and burns more wastefully. This last light variety is often teased out and used for the well-known peat moss-litter and peat moss-packing.

Before the reclamation of the large tracts of almost inaccessible "wild lands" one might almost put poaching beside the genuine wild-fowling and game industries. Bird lime, nets, decoys, almost every form of trapping besides the legitimate punt-shooting had their stronghold on the marshes.

> "Success to every gentleman that lives in Lincolnshire,
> Success to every poacher that wants to sell a hare,
> Bad luck to every gamekeeper that will not sell his deer.
> Oh, 'tis my delight on a shining night in the season of the year."
> *Old Song*

The fen drainage system is partly Roman, partly Anglo-Saxon, partly Dutch, and therefore completely English. The Bedford rivers take their name from the noble family who for generations wrought with gentleman adventurers for the drainage of the fens, and the Dutchmen have left their name and mark in many places. There is still a shop with the name of the Flemish painter, Van der Weyden, in March. One of the great difficulties was the isolating character of the land itself; communication across the fens before they were drained was only possible down tortuous routes, and the very character of the people bred under that icy east wind, stubborn, determined and aloof, made combined action well-nigh impossible, so that the draining system is particularly English in that a thing tackled so wrong-headedly—*works!* Probably handled, like giant works abroad, by an English modern engineering firm, it would have been much better done. As it is, commentors on the fen drainage system are divided into two schools; one says "Marvellous human enterprise!" and the other "What an ungodly mess." To those interested in engineering, one of the interestingly difficult points is that the peat shrinks so much after draining that the sluices which were originally dug to drain the water from the land are presently raised up high above the land they are supposed to drain, and the water has to be pumped up into them. These windmill pumps and ceaseless pumping engines are part of the fen land-

99 PAINTING THE WINDMILL, MORETON, ESSEX

98 INSIDE A WATER-MILL, HOUGHTON, HUNTINGDONSHIRE

100   MERRY-GO-ROUNDS AT A MIDDLESEX COUNTRY FAIR

scape. The great inundations, when the sea swept in over the dykes and up the low rivers, date from our earliest chronicles, so old that it is difficult to check their accuracy.

> "That flow strewed wrecks about the grass,
>   That ebbe swept out the flocks to sea;
> A fatal ebbe and flow, alas!
>   To manye more than myne and mee:
> But each will mourn his own (she saith);
> And sweeter woman ne'er drew breath
> Than my sonne's wife, Elizabeth."[1]

When the Croyland bells were broadcast, one heard more than the swinging sweetness of the bells, for within the trembling circles of sound were swept the space of open wind-swept sky, bending reeds, cry of wild-fowl on the marshes, the white foaming water under the night sky and flying clouds.

Those who know the Broads and Fen district as a popular summer holiday resort, picture the levels gay with white-winged sails and happy laughter, a land of blue skies and racing cloud shadows and sparkling water—and hampers sent down from Piccadilly. They glory in some of the most light-hearted holiday waters of England, in very pleasant care-free, summer days, but they do not know the wild fens of flood and storm, white silent frost and winter loneliness.

[1] J. Ingelow, *High Tide on the Coast of Lincolnshire.*

CHAPTER VI

DOWNS AND WOODS

"Chylturne grounde & flyntye grounde be light groundes, & drye & full of small stones, & chalke grounde is moche of the same nature. They wyl weare & washe awaye with water, & therefore they would be donged [dunged], as the bronze & fernye groundes be, for marle is seldome founde in these manner of groundes. Therefore, yf ye want shepe & donge, they wolde lye ley [i.e. fallow], & reste them, that they maye mende with lyenge."

FITZHERBERT'S *Husbandrie*, 1535

"BRITAIN is a green land and hath the name of Albion by reason of the white cliffs"; thus was our island known of old by its downland, and the downs of England are quite unlike any other country. If it is sound hypothesis that woodland, rock and earth-bound people become idolaters, and the sea coast and open desert breed abstract gods, then is the peace of the downs accounted for. These empty stretches of open green hill sweep across Southern England and end in the white chalk cliffs of the Southern coast; cliffs that may show misty white and pearl on a grey day to a ship beating up Channel, or gleam white as the billowing white clouds in the blue in sunny weather. Back in from the sea, the chalk hills roll on in smooth peaceful curves, steep or gentle, but always smooth, back to Butser Hill, highest point in Hampshire. Old Butser, white and green and bare, last of the Hampshire downs, rolls over the meeting-place of the great chalk mass of the central southlands, with the lines of the North Downs running north-east, and (to eastward) the beech-clad South Downs on their long course to the sea.

If you would know the grass downs of sheep-folds and peace, then I would send you to the very white heart of the chalk land, by Butser Hill, and from there you may walk eastward on to Cocking. You may go in the winter, when the fine small rain is sighing down on the grey grass, and the sea is a misty blur far away on your right, and the few hawthorn-trees are hung with rain on all their spikes. Or, if you go in summer, go at midsummer, at midday; then the sun is overhead, so there are no lights and shadows to come between you and the smooth modelling of that quiet land. The chalk downs are weathered to their curves by the filtering mist and rain and travelling

88

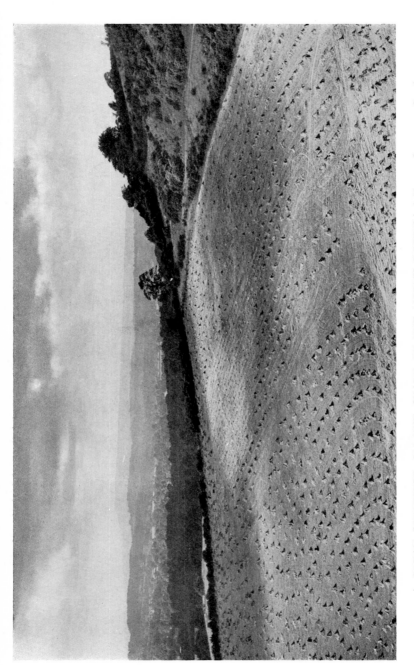

101 A GREAT CORNFIELD ON THE CHALK OF THE NORTH DOWNS : A Harvest Scene near Caterham

102 A SOUTHDOWN FLOCK OF THE CUCKMERE VALLEY, SUSSEX

wind. The restless earth is smoothed down as the curves of the sea are smoothed down from force to peace under rain.

At noonday walk quietly, mile beyond quiet mile, the grey-green of the down holding the very curve of the cloud above, the very sweep of the wind around. There will be no sound but bird song. . . . At noonday on the top of the downs, drop quietly on to the short soft turf, while the sun sheds down warmly, and a small wind runs through the grasses, and give your body to the round of the chalk; lie back at rest, out-flung arms and sprawling legs, adrift to the curve of the hill-side. Your shoulders, settling themselves against the gentleness of the yielding turf, press out the hot aromatic scent of the thyme, and the small grasses are sliding between empty open fingers. . . . Then, beyond a few centuries . . . through which drones a passing bee . . through the peace descended, the afternoon sunlight will presently fall lower, and warm into milky gold, and the shadows will lengthen over the curving downs. As the little warm earth wind stirs past your face, it will bring the "Tonk!" "Tonk!" of distant sheep bells . . .

Wake then! For a panting woolly sheep-dog will suddenly stand over you! And behind, quietly moving, there will be a grey soft flock of sheep. The nearest sheep will be standing still, little feet together, small heads and wide ears set in astonishment to see an intruder on their land; and, as their shepherd passes you, the sheep will turn and move on again—move and stop—as they crop—and the shepherd will smile kindly at your drowsing awakening, and make excuse that "the thyme in the grass is wonderful for sleep," but "look how the sea mist is now coming up the hill," and "he now is going back to the fold," but "if you were to follow down on the white track, to the bottom, he would ask her, and she would be putting the kettle on against your coming?"

(O blessed peace and friendliness of England's country! May there always be one who will "put the kettle on" against our coming back from dreams.)

The downland sheep are quite different from the hardy little mountaineers, or the fat placid sheep of the Midland plains: they are unlike the long-sided Flemish-faced Romney Marsh sheep, or the sturdy Shropshires. The Southdown ewes breed early in spring, while yet a flurry of snow is crisping over the short grass and drifting up in sweeps against the straw-set hurdle of the lambing pen. They lamb down in the bottoms. All lambs are delightful, but the littlest curly-woolled, flap-eared, splint-legged, bleating Southdown lambkin was the original toy that Mrs. Noah let the children have to

o

play with in the ark nursery on a wet day, and his portrait has
trailed about, on a green painted wooden stand, with a ribbon
round his neck ever since!—He is awfully good mutton later
on. It is the grazing flocks which go up on to the downs each
morning, and all day long crop and crop the short thymy grass,
or cluster round the dew pond. At night the downland sheep
return back to their folds in the fields below. They fatten
through the autumn, winter and spring, on hurdle-enclosed
turnip fields, or on the lower pastures, where armfuls of fodder
are flung down for them. Swedes don't suit the Southdown
apparently, but all sorts of green and clover crops and turnip
and mustard are grown for them, and sometimes they feed
them corn cakes (almost as much for the sake of the land as
the sheep, for the folding of the sheep upon the fallow crop
enriches the land for the following year's tilling).

The hurdles (64) are plaited on the wooded down and
are brought to the grass down, piled high on lorries, swaying
along the level white roads, to be dumped down in great
springing piles, at the ends of the turnip field where the sheep
are to be folded. Then comes the shepherd and his field man,
with stakes and a heavy wooden hurdle-mallet, and they look
at the hurdles, and they walk round the hurdles, and then they
go and look at last year's hurdles, that are already down in the
bottoms, and decide the new hurdles are as good as the old
hurdles, and then they look at the sky, and they look at the
lorry-man (and he goes back where he came from), and then
they set to work. The hurdles are laid down flat, spacing out a
section of the field. It may be this first section, for the first
feed is sometimes purposely thinned out, or some bags of hay
or green fodder laid down to break the change from short
grass to root diet, the arrangement of the folding having been
decided on beforehand. So the hurdles rise in a thin brown line,
with a shove of the foot and a tap of the mallet, and a binding
each to each. Then, while the wind blows down from the
hills, bringing the "tonk!" "tonk!" of sheep-bells, and the sun
sifts through the new hurdles, the men who have been working
between the rows of blue cabbage come in and join the hurdle
setters, and they find a sheltered corner in the new fold and
have their "noons," and come evening, the sheep come in.
The downs are a world that belongs to sheep craft, but a very
different world from the cold rock-bound sheep-walks of the
North, with their hard stone shelters and stone-slated stone-
stepped steadings.

There are barns on the downland (105), great grey timbered
ones; some of the timbers may have been part of a ship and felt

the wash of the sea, others bend their grey curved roots up-wards to a thatched roof, whose ties were new when the woods of the downs were cut for iron smelting. The thatch on a down-land barn is high pitched, dark and round and deep, and sweeps almost to the ground, and inside such a barn it is always evenly cool, neither hot in summer nor cold in winter. I found such a barn far west on the Wiltshire downs at the end of a hot summer. All the world was dry and cracked with heat, but I clambered up to rest in the strong comfortable fork of the ridge pole; all in the dusk under the thatch was cool and quiet, and a big brown owl opened two lamps at me, and shut them up again. The shearing had left the barn floor empty but for piled hay-padded sacks, upon which the reapers had knelt, and the yellow sunshine, washed in below the high open barn door, lay level as a pond. The gold light from below gilded the century-old tithe and tally marks, carved high on the grey curved beams; it hung gold buckles on the grey dusty leather harness against the walls, and gave a golden tongue to a sheep-bell, fast to its wooden yoke over a beam.

The dew ponds on the downs are still a mystery, and no one seems quite certain how they keep full. The old race of dew-pond makers is dying out, but the oldest pools are still full of quiet water. There is a grounding of flint and rock, and puddled clay and straw under a dew pond, and often a tree, if only a twisted thorn, leans up and hangs over the pond, but many are smooth round pools, like moon-pennies, lain on the green of the downs, and they stay full of water even in hot summer. The sheep-bells, many of them very, very old, belong to the shepherd, and as a rule have been in his family for years and years. They are difficult to get now, the old ones; one shepherd told me of tracking down a lost brother, who had gone abroad years ago and had come back, and in the end he found him and recovered a sheep-bell "back of him," that "had belonged in the set in his grandfather's time." He didn't know where the *brother* was now, *but the sheep-bell was in its place; on the downs!* The bells used to be swung on a wooden yoke that fitted round the neck of the sheep, and hung clear. The yoke rested against the shoulder bone. (I've seen the Lumbwa in Kenya make just such a yoke for their flocks.) Nowadays the bell often just swings loose on a leather thong. Sometimes you will find an old wooden yoke shoved away in a barn, or at the far back in an old brick oven in a farmhouse. We think it is true the sheep once swung their bells against the wolves, for long ago, when herdboy Watt skipped off to Bethlehem, did he not tell his dog to watch well, *and his wether to ring loud his bell?*

Sometimes a shepherd who "takes over for the season" will bring his bells with him; sometimes they "tonk!" "tonk!" and ring over the same pastures year after year.

The downland sheep-dog is often the great white woolly old English sheep-dog, with his sheep-coloured fleece and great clumsy paws. This powerful type is a great contrast to the small light fleet-foot black dog with a white tail tip, who leaps over the rocks on the mountains. The downland shepherd still uses a crook, the long five- or six-feet ash haft and iron-ended sheep crook, which would be too cumbersome for the mountain-walker. These crooks are, or were, made specially by a Sussex crook maker at Poynings under the hills. They must be about double the thumb thickness through the loop; I have seen some new ones made with a spring catch, but I have not seen them in use.

It was a shepherd of the downland sheep who taught me the making of a downland mutton's toilet. It was an interesting, half-humorous story. He had sold some sheep to a man, and "stuck out for his price," because the sheep were good meat: "It was really good stuff I was selling him," but they'd been "left" and were "looking none too good," so "after he'd paid and I was to deliver them next day, I was rather pleased with myself, getting that price," for they were an unkempt lot, "but I took them back and that night turned to and cleaned them up! I first put the hot shovel in the fire and ran it down their backs, for they had got a good fleece on then and it broadened them out, and then I trimmed them up with the shears, and pulled out the wool either side their faces, and cleaned up their ears, and washed their legs, and gave them an oiling. I gave them a good rest and drink over night, and next day when I took them in, he *was* surprised!—and pleased. 'Well,' he said, 'they look a better lot than I thought they were; I thought you were coming over me a bit with the price, but now I see I made a better bargain than I thought I had.' He well might say that for they were good meat and all of them cut up above the average weight I gave him. Next year I sold him some lambs straight from the teat,' and he said 'That's all right, it's a stiff price, *but they'll look handsomer when I get them in the market*. . .!' " They raddle some of the Southdown fleeces now, which process amuses some of the old shepherds very much. "Wash them?" grinned one shepherd. "In old times they would have been washed, and that's a fact; this is the first season I have ever been paid money for dut" (dirt, i.e. earth, raddle).

The old shepherds say it is no use trying to overcrowd the

103   A ROUND-UP IN THE CARMARTHENSHIRE HILLS

104 THE SOUTH DOWNS NEAR BRAMBER, SUSSEX

105 IN A WILTSHIRE VILLAGE: Coombe Bisset

pastures because next year at lambing time the losses will bring the flock down to the right number.

It is on the Downs, North and South, that are found those little round fossil sea-urchin things, which children call "shepherds' crowns." Alack! that even ghost shepherds should lose money on the downs!

There seems to be a possible new development on the chalk downs in experimental fur-breeding pens. A pen for mink, fitch, etc., has found this porous, quickly drained land very suitable, but this is only tentative at present.

Salisbury Plain belies its name, being anything but level. It has the wide open spacious character of your level plain land, but varies much in each different district. In places are rich arable fields, some of the whitest, creamiest barley you have ever seen; great tracts are grazing, other wide level patches are given over to mixed farming, and there are wide stretches of heath, given over to military manœuvres. I think one of the funniest things I ever saw plodding along a peaceful sunlit English road was a comfortable motherly soul, with the broad strong low-heeled shoes of the countrywoman, the wide clean white apron of unruffled afternoon, a flapping old-fashioned sun-bonnet and a heavy basket of eggs. She was walking steadily and comfortably along the quiet road, obviously waiting to be overtaken by the local bus. We passed the time of day, a lark lifted from the field and sang above us. Then suddenly with a din and a yell over the brow of the hill, crashing over the brushwood and plashing down upon us, there loomed a huge grey iron cambering tank, bristling with guns and vociferous with khaki. Automatically (expecting the bus) she hailed it, and the derision of the passing lads passed us down the road in a cloud of dust. She looked after it, she adjusted her bonnet, she caught my smile with a twinkle in her eye. "Well," she said, "I don't call that civil, but I would not have liked to have entrusted that vehicle with these eggs; they're for a setting."

The names of villages in the downland nearly all belong to the rare streams of chalk. Because of the porous nature of the subsoil, many streams and springs only run through some months, swiftly and clearly, while the underground water is at their level, and then cease, almost like turning off a tap. Winterbourne is such a name, and Lambourne and Hurstbourne.

The flints that are found in the chalk are not so valuable now (for glass flints, *see* Seacoast Section). The old work of the flint knappers is reduced to a single shed, where the last of the men still make enough small flints for the few flint-lock guns abroad, for lighters and for odd jobs. Fints newly quarried

P

must be used, as they are softer and fracture better. For the flints that are broken up for road metal, the old field heaps are better, being harder and fracturing more suitably.

The downland world is apart from the rest of England. Every curve of the chalk against the sky is different, and all the small flowers in the fields and the trees in the hedgerows are different from any other part of England. The colours are clearer and more delicate, and the scent of flowers and plants that grow in chalk is stronger and sweeter. That is why there are many small successful herb farms tucked away in the down country, and large plantations of essential oil plants such as lavender, mint, etc., do well in the chalk. The wild cherry-wood smells sweetly in the wet, and yew-trees, with a few dark lines showing almost black against the white, have their queer musky smell intensified. Some of the shrubs you will not get elsewhere in England, or only very rarely. The guelder rose, sweetbriar, and juniper grow wild, and all over the hedges hangs the grey dusk of traveller's joy, which will go with you far down through Wiltshire into Somerset. The little flowers of the chalk grow close, the rock rose and the bird's foot trefoil, but it is the orchids, the rare bee orchid, and the fly orchid (so incredibly lifelike) that are the most fascinating treasures to find. The thyme of the sheep-walks is shorter and less wiry than our hill-top thyme, and in the hedgerows, along the bottoms are wild parsley, the white bladder campion, blue chicory, and the larger scabious, which is neither pink, blue nor lavender, but the colour of the mist that lies over the sea on a hot August afternoon.

Many of the herbs of the downs are used for medicine, and are gathered and sent away to be dried, or prepared over the fire in the farmhouse down below the hill.

Of the great ironworks that were once the industry of the country under the downs, nothing remains but a few single workshops and the derelict ponds here and there. Sometimes even the slag heaps have been cleared for road metal. The charcoal burner is practically gone from the downs; he worked midway between the wooded downs and the open lands, for his charcoal was needed by the hop growers. Now the hop growers use coal and anthracite with their faggots, and many of the most up-to-date oast houses are arranged so that the hot air only goes up from the furnace house. So the charcoal burner is now very, very rare, and it is only old people who will tell you of the round wood fires he made, stacked so skilfully, covered over with earth, and then watched, day and night, while the wood smouldered, and the pile sank, slowly, while he

106 HARROWING THE SPRING PASTURES AT WEST SHEFFORD, BERKSHIRE

107   THE " LIFT " AT WORK ON SALISBURY PLAIN

patched up the cracking earth, and shifted round his hurdle and sacking wind screen, to suit the slow-passing draught. Only the charcoal burners' ghosts will stay for ever, burning charcoal in the beechwoods on the downs, for here and there on a still day, when there is no cloud or no mist about, a little thin thread of smoke will be seen, mounting up and up through the beechwoods, as if one watched at a banked-up fire there . . . and you may mark the spot, and you may go, go at once and quickly, but you will never find anyone there. And these single mysterious threads of smoke or mist which no one has ever satisfactorily explained away are called "the colyers."

Coming down off the grey-green chalk downs into the Sussex Weald, and sometimes in Kent and Essex, the sheep hurdles may be replaced by thick shelters made of straw, drawn straw, set upright in a hurdle frame, especially in cold bleak fields, where the wild east wind whistles across the Channel. This straw may be specially grown for thatching straw, or it may be from locally grown Sussex oats. Sussex oats have made a name for themselves, though some say it's more in the grinding than in the oats. They are a mixture of oat and barley; the whole oat, including the husk, is ground up with about one-tenth part barley. It is ground in different thicknesses, and some of the finest grindings are used by the Sussex poultry fatteners, who are so handily placed for sending fat poultry to the London market, or liver wings to Brighton.

The ploughs of the downland are utterly different from those of the Midland or the North. They are as individually localised as the wooden plough of Essex or the Norfolk plough. The Sussex and Kent ploughs are again both quite different from those used in the Western and Hampshire bottoms, or on the North Downs. All downland ploughs seem still to hold the old oxen-draught condition in their design. They have the slower longer line of the heavy widely turning oxen in their make, but they are locally adapted for the very varied tillage. The Kentish plough, still in use in many places, is almost the old high "hoe plough" described by Tull. The superstructure and draught end of the forebeam is raised so high on two even axle wheels that the pendant coulter and sheath appear to "reach down" to the furrow from above, and appear designed to scratch along the surface, rather than plough it. On the other hand, the wooden "slide beam" to which the iron share is attached, and the moulding board, if any, is so long, wide and cumbersome that it might at first glance be mistaken for the rough wooden sledges upon which some Northern ploughmen transport their iron ploughs along the stony highways of the North.

But, as the sea shapes ships, so the soil shapes the plough-share, and this apparently cumbersome structure will work steadily long after a lighter metal plough has succumbed to a sudden attack of flints.

On the comparatively dry, and almost too quickly drained land of shallow surface soil, the plough must go deeply through the tilth, but should leave the subsoil as compact as possible, making, in country parlance, a "firm seed bed," or a "good footing, under grain and green." Perhaps one reason for the preservation of this type of plough, especially towards Kent, is its definite value when working between crops, or along rows that need pressing in. The last plough oxen of England belonged to the Down country, and as surely does the Down country plough belong to the oxen. There is an affinity between the slow, steady strong draught of a long ox line with the wide sweeping headlands and steady continuous strength, and the quiet strong rounded hills of the chalk—they have the same movement.

THE WOODED DOWNS

Beech-trees grow well all over the downland country, but the North Downs hold a world full of grey and brown beech-woods, miles of beechwoods, only broken here and there into small open clearings, where the wild cherry-tree blossoms in the spring, and the scented wood violets make small drifts of purple among the crinkling beech leaves. These rounded downlands tilt up and down into mounded hills, and have small farmsteads tucked down among the hollows (60). The little tilted fields wear out more ploughs and cultivators to the square acre than anywhere else in England, on account of the flints. Flints as "big as your head, and about as ugly; flints as small as your tongue, and about as sharp." The great beech-trees that stand over the downs seem to own the district, and only permit a few humans to live among them, and those human must be carefully pegged down in small brick and timber cottages in the clearings.

Twice in the year you must visit the beechwoods on the downs. In the spring the new green beech leaves are silky soft, so translucent they hardly hold a shadow, only drop pools of green light around the silver tree trunks, and drifts of bluebells cover all the ground with azure. There are two things that everyone born English should surely have a right to see for ever. The Devon daffodils, bobbing and dancing in the spring sunshine, and the bluebells swaying under the green shaded beech-trees.

The second visit to the beechwoods must be in the autumn. Then, among the flaming gold of the foliage, the grey beech trunks show blue as smoke. On autumn days there falls a patter of rain over the curled brown leaf drift, and the green moss in the woods is inches deep and redolent with that sweet elusive penetrating scent, which is not quite ferns and not quite violet leaves—and not quite wet earth and winter coming, but a fronded soft scent that holds a little of them all.

Among the undergrowth will be growing all sorts of exciting small fungus, the "inky tops," which are good to eat, the white *suède* and brown-sealskin furry fungus and the tiny dew-filled scarlet frilled cups, which of old were dried and ground up into powder, and used as opium, to give strange dreams. The witches' butter will be oozing and dripping from the underbush in rich clots of gold juice. In some woods are morels, if you're lucky enough to find them. Besides the great beechwoods of well-grown trees, the downland has large copses of undergrowth. These hazel and ash thickets used to be fairly valuable, or in some places young Spanish chestnuts were grown in quantities for hop poles before the modern use of larch and stretched wire. They are still found on the Sussex sandy heights, and hurdles are made from them on the spot.

In the bottoms, and by pools, a little alder is grown for special uses. This damp-proof wood was sold to the powder mills for making boxes for ammunition. In the North it was used for bottoms of clogs. Now, the scarlet whips stand up like a fire which is lighted by the water-side.

These underwood copses are not very high and, save where an oak shadows overhead, there will be miles and miles of brushwood, just low enough for the sunlight to come filtering through, so that, in spring, the ground below will be carpeted with violets and primroses, while overhead shake the long tassels of the yellow catkins and the tiny shining scarlet of the hazel nut. Through these sunlit woods, the small birds tip-tilt up-and-down, with little sweet swift calls, or snatches of song; companies of little upside-down tom-tits will be catching the sunlight, looking as if the primroses and the violets themselves had taken wings; or a robin will be singing up in the alder after rain and a slim-headed thrush jumping backwards, and pecking between his toes among the brown leaves. There are dormice and sometimes, very rarely, a red squirrel, but the grey squirrels have chased them nearly all away. Perhaps, as you go through the wood, you will see a white blaze cut on a tree, and another farther on, and you will mark the place where presently you may come back and sit by the woodcutter's fire.

It is surprising the number of interesting people doing curious things in the beechwoods. Passing along the road over the downs, you'd never suspect anything was going on. No advertisement, no fuss, you would never know that perhaps a few hundred yards away quite a number of people were very busy, quietly getting on with their jobs.

No factory, no company, no red tape—sometimes it's a small one-man show, sometimes twenty or thirty are employed. You cannot lay down any regulations about *the way* it is done, because each worker unit is a separate individual enterprise, and most of the workers hold to their own British right to be independent and aloof, and do their own work as they want to do it and not, as one of them expressed it, be "badgered about." A large number of chair-workers have succumbed to mass production and now work in factories, according to prearranged commercial considerations, and I suppose the evolution is inevitable in all branches, yet there were never better chairs made than those wooden chairs made in the beechwood. They were turned, as they are still in the Chilterns, on an old pole lathe in the shed; they were structurally sound and very strong and comfortable. The tradition was to make them entirely of beech wood, though I possess some whose seats are oak. A very special sort are sometimes made from the wild cherry, but the workers did not often sell these; they'd turn up a set themselves when they were getting wed. The wood has a fragrance that comes out strongly in damp weather. Most of this chair-work now has become localised round High Wycombe.

Plenty of other work still gets done in the woods, but you'd be hard put to tell a stranger where to find it. The country people know, but like all country people they admit to knowing more than they say, and many of the camps can only be reached on foot and there is no track until after the job is finished, when a way is broken out for the lorry, which will lurch and crash through and fetch the goods away. Maybe a couple of bicycles, leaning behind a tree, where no bicycle should be, or perhaps a curl of chip-wood sticking in the mud of a footprint, or perhaps a distant, insistent, woodpecker noise, carrying down through the green on some quiet summer afternoon. Whatever the clue, if you follow, it will lead you through the woods to a small camp of woodworkers, working away through rain, hail or sunshine, in the middle of the forest. All sorts of things are made; tent pegs, clog bottoms, the backs for scrubbing brushes, wooden blocks for wheel-brakes, wheelbarrows, ladders, etc.; the tools will be of the simplest, usually the woodworkers' old foot vice will be in use. Every sort of woodworker uses this;

108, 109   BARREL-MAKING IN ASHDOWN FOREST

it's simple enough, holds with the shove of the foot and leaves both hands free to work. There will be some tree boles, sawn down for use as chopping blocks, and each man will have fixed up his own few, very simple tools. There will be a grindstone, probably trundled in by hand; there may be an old tin bath, or tub, for water supply; there will be an iron hook to boil the kettle, a neat fire of chips; and there will be a dog, to tell them if anyone is coming. There will be a shed, and this will probably have pegs knocked up inside to hang up your coat, and a nail to hang up somebody's watch to keep the time by, and there will usually be a box and a bottle or two and a tin of sugar and a shelf on which to put the "bits of things you don't want to lose," and altogether the little workshop in the woods will have accumulated unto itself all the "odd things a chap wants," and "none of the things he doesn't." The roof of the shed is usually a couple of sheets of corrugated iron. If they're conversational chaps that don't like the noise when it rains, they'll probably have thrown up a pretty deep covering of chips; or if it gets hot, with the sun on top, they'll do the same thing, or sometimes, if it's a "stripping job," there'll be heaps of limp stringy bark and bundles of twigs all over the top of the hut so that it looks like a muffled-up porcupine suffering from bronchitis.

It looks jolly comfortable too when the boy (there's always "the boy") has made up the fire, and got the kettle singing, and the billycans all ranged round and the teapot (that's the boss's) warming, and it's about four o'clock, and the sun beginning to tilt down westward. It's less pleasant when a hail-storm rattles down and everything gets cold and wet, but on the whole, the workers *would rather be out where they are most of the year* and they can't work long in the winter, the woods aren't right.

The *underwood* workers on the whole move about more swiftly, and are seldom more than a month or so in any one coppice, but their sheds and tools, and packing, and the chip-wood fire and kettle, are all there the same. Palings and stakes for hurdles, and all manner of "straight work" are cut in the underbush. A woodman's grip that's made with two stout logs of wood and a length of flexible wire is used for wedging together bundles of hurdle stake or palings, until they are secure, either with wire, or a strip of bark, etc. I've seen a couple of bucket handles nailed to four stakes, and used as a convenient "bundle gauge," and, for length, a couple of barrels sunk in the ground sort the stakes thrown into them, as quickly as any other way. Sometimes a young sapling will be bent down and fastened with a noose to a log, the natural spring thus made acting as a vice. There's no end to the primitive and simple ingenuity of the woodworker.

The pioneer men clearing the coppice have no need of a bucket fire of chips, for they must burn off the trimmings of their job as they go along. The twiggy thin brushwood is piled up, started with a handful of chippings, or a faggot from the last fire, and puffs off swiftly in one crackling blaze that subsides rapidly and leaves a ring of stub ends in a perfect circle round a hearth of soft white ash. Walking round, the woodman shoves them into the centre again with his foot, and this time the thicker pieces burn more slowly. . . . All through the night, long after dusk has fallen and the workman has gone back home to his yellow firelit kitchen and tea . . . all night, the grey line of smoke from the woodman's fire mounts up and up, and in the morning the last white ashes of the outer stumps are smouldering out among the violet leaves. . . . Next rain the white circle will be black charcoal. Next spring a small black scar on the ground, over which the small greenwood plants are quietly creeping back.

Water is a problem on the high downs; on the grass pastures dew ponds are made. Sometimes small ponds can be made at a wood-side, but the porous chalk drains very quickly, and the small dykes and ditches are inadequate. Wells have to be sunk to a great depth; there is a well presented by the Maharajah of Benares for the inhabitants of Stoke Row, near Reading, which is 330 feet deep. Cottages have rain-water butts when the roofs are tiled, and one or two charcoal burners have had odd jobs supplying the gravel and charcoal water filters for private houses on the downs. Where a pump is fixed, as on a farm for cattle, it is an awfully long job pumping the water up, though it's thoroughly good when you get it.

The purity and clearness of the under-chalk water, where you can get it in the bottoms, give the downland country its somewhat specialised growing of watercress (76). Watercress, from very far back, has been rather an English speciality in salads. At a time when lack of winter feeding made the medieval farm calendar lop-sided, and salted and dried meats filled the winter menu, any natural antidote like watercress would be very serviceable. The few old-fashioned "greens" that we have in use in England have a very firm hold on the country mind, and continue traditionally popular, so that long after the countryman has become immured in cities, he still likes watercress to his tea. Most of the watercress consumed in London comes from the clear chalk streams of the downland; some comes from as far away as the Wiltshire Downs. The supply of water-cress is a pretty definite "chalk" industry—the best beds are those made around an artesian well, through the chalk. Now watercress cannot be cleansed or treated in any way without spoiling its "fresh" character, and if gathered from the country brook, where cows trudge across, or sheep come down to drink, it is definitely less clean than that which is grown directly round these clear fresh springs. From the artesian well the water bubbles up icy cold and pure, and ripples away through the green cress, and there grows as clean and whole-some a salad as you will get in England. The natural line of the stream is often spaced out into cement-lined pools that can be cropped in rotation, and where the depth can be regulated to get that short close spriggy crop, which is the green height of elegance in watercress. Towards the end of the season the plant is apt to get leggy; in midsummer the sun gives it a bronzing and by the time the little white flowers are beginning to show, water-cress is getting *passé*. The men wear waders to cut it and gather it into bundles (76); the cress is then bass-wrapped into its characteristic tight bunches, packed in shallow green baskets and railed up to town. Country people set great store by watercress —"They reckon it's a good thing to eat in the spring, they prophesy it purifies the blood." The right country way to eat it is to have a big plate of fresh bread and butter, a big dish of cress and a bowl of salt, and then you just go on until you think you've really got to stop. In restaurants it garnishes brown birds and flutters round fish. Medicinally, country herbalists make much use of watercress, expressing the juice from the strongest coarse growth as well as the leaves, and either beat it into hog's lard or work it up with fine oatmeal. Sometimes they bruise the watercress directly into the melted lard and make a green salve.

One joy of the downs is the horses. Many of our horse breeding and training stations are on the downs, and a long string of horses out exercising, or practising gallops over the green turf, will match the chasing shadows for lightness and speed. Large stables made a demand for corn and straw and a certain amount of local labour, but on the whole "the training stables" live a life apart in the country life around, and the invasion of the countryside for a big race belongs to the town almost more than to the country.

THE SAND "HEATHS" OF THE HILL AND DOWN COUNTRY

The Bagshot sand formation close to the downland section of England is a complicating factor in choosing characteristic landscape. For these commons (59) stretch right across the country, up into Hampshire, and though of comparatively low altitude, are true heath country, having black peaty sand and growing heath and Scotch firs; these districts give a mountain look and smell to the landscape. From the rustling beechwood on the curve of the Sussex downs one can look across brimming green bottoms, where cows graze and roots grow, straight across to a stretch of heather country, with yellowish sandy streaks and dark clumps of pine. In places along these sands there are wide stretches of planted rhododendrons, blue and purple, green and bronze, and larch plantations, with their soft green feather tassels. There are residential sections, such as Woking, with shrubberies, stretches of "forest" with deer, and stretches of forest with car parks, and stretches of parks with cars, and golf courses, and the well-known Richmond and Epping Areas near London. But there are unchanged heaths such as White of Selborne describes near Petersfield, where gipsies camp in tattered peace, and there are curved steeps that hold the golden afternoon sun, such as the golden warm brew that floods the Devil's Punchbowl, when the tiny yellow butterflies, like slips of lemon peel, and the curling gold bracken bronzes through the purple heather. This section of England continuing on to the Pilgrim's Way, and down into the hop gardens, where the East-enders come in autumn, was dedicated surely by Chaucer himself to Londoner's peace for ever, for they claim it in the same way that Lancashire, from Liverpool upwards, spills into the Lakes, the Potteries spill into North Wales, Sheffield and its peers own Kinderscout and Dovedale, and Notts, Leicester and the Midlands go to Mabelthorpe and Skegness, when they go to heaven.

III TILLING BULBS IN THE SCILLY ISLES

112 WINTER IN ASHDOWN FOREST

113 EARLY DAFFODILS IN CORNWALL

114   LONG SANDS AND CRAWLING WAVES IN NORTH DEVON

CHAPTER VII

SEACOAST AND ESTUARIES

"England is the most island of Ocean, and is beclipped all
about by the sea, and departed from the roundness of the
world, and height sometimes Albion: and hath that name of
white rocks, which were seen on the sea cliffs.

"England is a strong land and a sturdy, and the plenteousest
corner of the world, so rich a land that unneth it needeth help
of any land, and every other land needeth help of England.
England is full of mirth and of game, and men oft times able
to mirth and game, free men of heart and tongue, but the hand
is more better and more free than the tongue."

                                                    From an old Writer

WITH a long part of our sea line it is as difficult to decide where
the land ends and the sea begins, as it is to decide in this book
which section belongs to Coast and Estuaries and which to Fens
and marshlands. In a book, as in reality, they are bound to overlap. Therefore for the purpose of description I have considered
as "land" all marshes, flats, etc., which are of alluvial deposit,
that is ground which is essentially of earthy constituents, as
contrasted with the sea marshes and new land left by the
retreating sea.

The alluvial deposit land, in the estuaries of the rivers, is
naturally very fertile. It is the piled-up surface earth washed
down from higher inland, and therefore the resultant level or
marsh will be something similar to the land higher up stream
in ingredients, though arranged levelly and evenly mixed. These
flats become agricultural land under the turn of the plough.

The drowned river valleys of the East Coast and grass-
covered grazing sands of the West and the new earth-covered
sweeps of shingle (such as that near Dungeness) all confuse the
issue. Whatever distinction is obvious to the geologist, to the
average traveller these parts seem as loosely held between
land and water as the tide-washed hawthorn stumps on the
crumbling banks of the Stour, which grow blossom on one
branch and trail seaweed over the other, in a "pull-angel
pull-devil" between the tide.

These drowned valleys are obviously land sea-swamped;
the sand is sodden earth and there are more river- than sea-
shells, and the queer green growth particular to this type of
land sprouts up between stones which are still angular from

their earthy beds, and along the tide-washed drift old plough-shares and ships' paddles rust together among the decayed fish-nets and cabbage stalks.

There is about them more nearly a river estuary character; you will find grass lands and ploughed fields dropping to the very edge of the water, and the movement of the river can be tracked out as it sways from side to side.

I had reason to explore one such estuary near Harwich under the guidance of very old maps. The old sea wall that stood high and dry in some places was altogether washed away in others. In some places flat beaches of shingle and mud already covered with a low green growth lay like doorsteps below the fields, in other places the hedges ran straight out and perished in the water. One water-lapped field was marked in the fifteenth-century "Monastery"; in the sixteenth-century "Ruins of Monstery"; in the seventeenth-century "Site of old Chapel." When I located the spot in the twentieth century I stood and watched the peaceful sunshine and the wind stir a wide smooth field of barley, soft as ruffled cream. Impossible to break into that white gold peace, so I sought out the neigh-bouring farm. No, no ruins, no stones. Stay! the boy had found some stone steps in the wood, smugglers' steps probably, when he was after rabbits. With spade and pick, nettle-stung and briar-clawed we dug out the half-buried steps; they showed below the traces of fine cusping, as of a window! "Well, old Jarge was right then—we reckoned this field was called Martlebones on account of the Martello towers, but old Jarge at the George, he stuck us out it was Martyr-bones field—— He gets his pint!" (On the whole I should not say the English countryman was a natural antiquarian, but father to son he remembers a long time.)

The tidal flats are of different character, stretching away softly into the misty blue of the dusk, or sparkling hard and bright as a polished silver tray, set with green glass in the sun and wind. Often on the long level grey-green stretches the sea lies far out of sight and sound; only at high water the pools fill full, and at low they drain empty. At the turn of the tide, through the muddy dykes, come gurgles and sobs, and all the soft voices of rising water. So mournful are the salt marshes in the dusk of a winter evening; the shadowform of earth is lost; only sea birds scream above in the void, there is a sighing in the mist, and the water voices are almost human in their low sorrowful sound. Sometimes with the tide comes the wind, and moans over the marshes, and brings a soft dampness which hangs in tears on your eyelashes and chokes your breath, and

115   SAND-DUNES ON THE CORNISH COAST, NEAR HAYLE

116 LOW TIDE ON THE COAST OF YORKSHIRE

from the ground there rises a cold, which is like the cold of the grave and sinks into the very bone.

They used to grow opium poppy for ague on some of our wet lands. Tusser, our sixteenth-century farmer, speaks of the fever of Essex marshes, and some of the Northern marshes had a name for the same complaint till comparatively recently. In one place an enterprising Englishman is now attempting reclamation by planting rice.

Quite different from the land-locked estuary or the ghost-haunted tidal flats are the sand-dune lands. They too can be grave and mysterious, but they can also be the finest play-grounds. The broad long level green-covered sands of Harlech are a cheerful golf-course, bungalows be-dyked and barred by walls of sand-dunes, scented with thyme and haunted by children's laughter all through the summer holidays.

Then there are the Anglesey dunes, where they cut the marram grass, and the sand-dunes at Perranzabuloe that bury our first tiny English church. It is among the shifting, changing sand-dunes that the great winds come to rest, and you may watch them on a winter evening stir and sweep, making their beds, whirling the tossing sand and settling down with little stirrings and smoothings, and there go bendings of the long pliant dune grass, where invisible feet pass over out to sea.

There is surely nothing, not even excepting snow, so tiring to walk over as loose sand-dune—nor such fun to tumble and play over, with such warm sun-filled cups to sleep in, when the sea groans far below and the deep blue sky lies down on the ring of blue grey marram overhead. But sand-dunes grey and wet in an autumn wind are desolate places; the rain pits the sand and skins it with dusty webs, and the wet hard grass cuts through skin and ankle.

One industry of the sand-dunes is rabbit trapping. The traps are set lightly buried in sand to nip off leaping front paws, or crush the strong back legs. By law the steel traps must be visited once between sunrise and sunset, then the rabbit is "stretched" (i.e. jerked out and neck dislocated) and gutted and piled in flat bales and sent to the town market. By law—*between sunrise and sunset*—but have you ever walked over a warren when the traps are full, and their screams tear the stillness?—Or had the tortured little red and brown thing jerk itself blindly across your feet?

Summer resorts are truly a part of our coast line that violate all geological classification! They stand armed behind embattled sea fronts of concrete, pier bedight, and even resort to the transplanting of sand. Most of the popular ones have the

R

natural advantages of good beach and sheltered climate, or are the result of the proximity of overcrowded urban districts. Except in a few cases, they are astonishingly seasonal. In summer, crowded to a laughable extent, they appear large towns with theatres, music halls, cinemas and the rest. Then the piers and all the attractions are in full swing, and every shop is a-flutter with bathing towels and gowns, emergency party frocks and white flannels. Sand shoes cluster round their doors like parti-coloured bunches of strange rubber fruit. Along the front the shops bristle with children's spades and toys, and the air is a nice mixture of petrol, ozone and hilarity. Every second shop is a café, and the way to the station is lined with memento stalls. Donkeys and ponies earn their living on the beach, speed-boats and row-boats and fishing boats earn it in the bay, and there's hardly a person in the place who isn't putting his whole mind to the business of getting or spending.

But in winter you wouldn't know the same town—rows of shuttered grey houses and closed shops. Dilapidated dance halls draped with limp palls of peeling posters; closed rinks shudder. The east wind blows over desolate sands, where, drifted among the weed of winter storm, rot the bathing shoes of last summer. A few southern sheltered places in the warm South stay awake through the twelve months, and shelter a hibernating brood of Anglo-Indians and ex-colonials, who cower down there together for warmth in November, and play bridge over Christmas. For the shivering tropical palms on the parade stand up well enough against the blue sky, if there is a warm radiator and a sheet of steam-heated plate glass between the sun worshipper and the east wind.

COAST INDUSTRIES

Many of the English summer resorts are tucked away under the shelter of a cliff, but on the whole the cliff coast line of England is bare and rugged, with little industry save quarrying, or precarious bird and egg collecting on long swinging ropes down the face of the rock; some of the rocky islands are bird sanctuaries, others shelter lobster pots.

What's fish on some coasts, is no account on others. There are at least two dozen different sorts of shell fish eaten around England, but hardly any three are considered edible in the same locality. With the exception of whelks and winkles (when my nerve came off on the pin), I have eaten them all, and mostly they are very good.

Oysters are the best, of course—since Caesar. With the first

117 A CORNISH ESTUARY : The Fowey at St. Winnow's

118 SOUTH WALES COCKLE-WOMAN

119   THE FISH-CART AT ST. IVES, CORNWALL

120   FISHING-CRAFT IN NEWLYN HARBOUR, CORNWALL

121   BOAT-BUILDING AT CONYER, KENT

"R" in the month the oyster always appears in the Press News. "Picture of the Mayor and the First Oyster of the Year." (The Mayor is wearing his chain.) It was of an oyster patty an unknowing American said sadly: "Say, Bo—something's *died* in my bun." English oysters are well cared for; they are born in beds and planted out, and tended lovingly from the spawn to the lemon juice, and they have their headquarters at Whitstable and Colchester.

Cockles come next in popularity in the South; mussels, perhaps, in the North. Cockles are a trade at Leigh-on-Sea, where there are rows of cockle sheds beside great middens of empty shells. The cockle boats sail out and fetch the cockles off the sandbanks, the cargo is carried ashore, in "pad" baskets swung on wooden yokes over plank gangways, the planks well strewn with broken shell to give a grip to rubber seaboots. In the sheds the cockles are steamed open, winnowed from their shells, dumped in brine, and are eaten at oilcloth covered tables on the spot. The Leigh-on-Sea cockles are very small and rather sandy. Londoners like them, and take them home in bags. We like the large ones best, the cockles that are scratched up with an old rake or curry comb in the sandy estuaries, or spudded for on "flats." The cockle women (118) who used to inhabit Grange-over-Sands, the Severn Estuary, and certain localities on the East Coast, were an indomitable, sturdy race. Their large bare feet splayed out over the sands, they wore their husbands' trousers rolled up to the knees, and overhung them with voluminous thick skirts. The top one of these skirts was drawn forwards between the legs, and bundled up under a large leather strap which went round the waist. The frontal upholstery thus supplied was very imposing, and when they carried a good-sized pail on each arm and a rake before them, they had a Presence. Mostly large parties of cockle-gatherers would arrange for the panniered donkeys, or a little tilt cart, to come down to the shore and collect their bags at the end of the day, and the cockle party usually stopped for a warming nip at the inn on the way back. Nearly every little sandy bay or estuary around England has a solitary aloof cockle-gatherer pottering about individually. The families of Wells-next-the-Sea, Norfolk, turn out in force on Sunday afternoons and dig their splendid sands for cockles with industrious success. Some people like a roundish middle-sized black cockle; in Anglesey they often get a very large cockle as much as two inches across, and if you find the right inn, they will make you a deep creamy juicy cockle pie, with a crisp potato crust on top (very savoury). In some places the small cockles, dried off with oatmeal, are fried along with bacon, crisp and brown. Mussels are popular in the Black Country, and are good, hot on toast, with black pepper. Limpets are very local; the last place I heard of their being systematically gathered was the Isle of Man. Scallops are well known, expensive and rightly considered a delicacy. A long oval fish, locally called clam, is gathered in Norfolk and a few other places, but I have never found it for sale; it is collected often as a by-product by the cockle folk—as one gatherer explained: "They would be all of an oyster, if a chef had them, but we keep them to eat ourselves." Razors, again, are very local. Only a few old folk, usually islanders settled on the mainland, seem to know them. Where you get a good many there is usually somebody locally who knows *to* them. Whelks and winkles belong to the town stall and the naphthalene lamp.

Shrimps are netted, and a shrimping net is one of the finest nets that are made. The beam of a shrimping net is anything up to six feet wide and the pole from twelve to fourteen feet long. The cross bar rests against the thighs, and shoved along, with an action something like "Devonshiring" on land. Prawns are quite different, and are baited for in prawn nets; but are really so superior they are more akin to lobster. Lobsters are caught in lobster pots, of type differing in various localities. The French take over all our Irish lobsters by the season. Years ago out on an island off the West coast, we could get nothing to eat for weeks but lobsters, which averaged fivepence to ninepence each. Being young and hungry, we had a lobster apiece, some hot pan bread and a good strong cup of tea every night for supper and slept in peace, but later a lady novelist came over "collecting local colour" and brought patent foods (and sandals and cold cream), so she was rather a problem. Said I: "Colleen, you can't feed that grown-up woman on lobsters and tea at 10 p.m.; she will curl up and die on you." "And why?" replied the hospitable colleen, "What harm is there in a lobster? Faith, there is a lot of miscellaneous eating on a lobster! Sure, with a lobster and a good cup of tea she'll come to no harm till morning." (And by the grace of St. Patrick, she didn't.) In England we are more respectful about lobsters, for we have fewer. Crabs now are common, and we often have roast crab for tea. Dressed crab is very good eating, but there are parts in the North where they wouldn't look at one, no, nor countenance a shrimp! We *are* individual in our choice!

The seaweed of our coast used to be more important than it is now. In times when it was used as a manure its value was considerable, so great that it entered to the rent accounts of

123 STAITHES: A Steep-stepped Fishing Village in Yorkshire

many farms. Sometimes it was burnt, and the ashes used as top dressing; more often the weed itself was carted inland and "ploughed under" in furrows. After storm the weed-gatherers, bare-foot and bare-armed, would pile the weed up on to the backs of donkeys, or into great creels that were hauled up the cliff face by men with ropes above. Sometimes carts with boarded barrel wheels (see note in "Flats and Fens") would trundle down to some small bay and the weed be carted inland, but the long brown and gold kelp weed was gathered chiefly off the rocky coasts. In the Scilly Isles the "vreack" harvest was cut and dragged from the rock in a wet laughing sea-festival in March. The burning for kelp and soap products is practically obsolete now in England, though still an industry of the Western islands.

A local weed called laver is gathered in some parts. It is like thin brown silk clinging to the rocks between tide-marks. It used to be a great delicacy. In the days when Bath was at the height of its popularity the street cry of the laver woman travelled far inland. Laver is served hot with mutton in Devon to-day. It is scraped from the rocks into baskets, washed, boiled and served hot with melted butter, or tangerine orange juice, or sometimes eaten cold like pickles. Laver belongs to the "marsh" mutton of the saltings, just as thyme belongs to the lean mountain mutton, and red currant jelly belongs to the valley fat mutton.

A white seaweed (the carrigean of the Irish) is locally known as "Dorset weed," "white weed," and to the chemists as Iceland Moss or Irish Moss. This is a vegetarian gelatine with many uses, as for instance forming the foundation for the marbled printing of end papers, the substance of cough jujubes, and the basis of many delicious blancmanges and jellies—it keeps the soused herring in countenance, and upholding false teeth! and is still used by some chemists in preference to gum tragacanth in the making of cod-liver oil emulsion. The weed gives a less white preparation, but is considered a better product.

Samphire that grows on the sand-dunes is pickled by the country people. Like many country specialities, it has never been commercialised, but continues to be gathered and used for generations, through conservative family custom. You may find a few jars in a local pannier-market, but it is seldom for sale in shops.

One of the oldest trades lies hidden among the sand-dunes. Here, in the autumn, come the women who cut the marram grass and bind it in swathes and leave it to *won*, after which it is

s

carted back and stored in sheds. All through the long winter months they plait mats and hassocks and chair seats, and all manner of things out of the grey-green grass, which is almost imperishable. All the Western rick covers used to be of marram grass, for hay below marram seldom "heated," which in a damp climate is important. A trial has been made of using the long plaited strips, instead of straw, to lay between the lines of strawberry plants. Good brooms and brushes are made of the stronger grasses and sell locally for a few pence each.

One of the curious spasmodic industries along the pebbly parts of the coast is flint picking. The round black flints are gathered from the shore, piled into trucks and railed inland to the glass factories. The first time I saw half a dozen men, with half a dozen baskets, kneeling down and putting five miles of shingle beach one at a time into small round baskets, I thought I had really reached the last English industry! But this is still the easiest way of getting the flint they want for glass making.

They used to gather cuttle fish for the makers of tooth pastes and coach-work polishers, but it is imported now, because the people who use it for getting a surface on motor-car paint want larger pieces. There are shops in Soho where the windows are piled high with masses of the white friable stuff. The "darts" or pencil-like bones of the ancient little squids occur in crowds in the Dorset cliffs, a witness to the swarming myriads of these decapods in the primeval seas. After a heavy storm piles of cuttlefish strew the shores in some parts, and they may be bought cheaply in London. With special treatment in cooking they can be quite moderately palatable, but in unskilled hands the result is tougher than the closest india-rubber.

*　　*　　*　　*　　*

The highest rocks of England occur naturally in the mountainous districts, and therefore come with the Mountain Section.

The hills of the Lakes sweep down to foothills, and have level lands lapping out to sea; the isolated red cliffs of the East Coast break off direct from the corn lands, so that the plough turns perilous headlands by the crumbling edge, and yellow corn and red poppies stand up sheer against the blue. The crumbling of this red cliff beyond Norwich has set the sites of whole villages out to sea, and made the soft red cliff face a happy hunting ground for the geologist and archaeologist. This ruinous demolition has its humorous side—when you pass along the front of charming villas which state "To Let" in the front windows, but on going around behind there isn't anything there but a strip of wall paper fluttering out to sea. As recently as last winter the falls by Lowestoft necessitated a whole row of cottages turning out and moving farther inland.

At the end of Carnarvonshire, on the extreme West there is a cliff of jasper; whole farmhouses and barns are built of jasper. By St. David's head, the great black cliffs sweep in wide jagged-edged slants down to sandy coves, which shelter happy bathing parties all through the summer holidays. Parts of Pembrokeshire are called "little England beyond Wales" and have the most intricate and curious history. From the time of Flemish inundation during our own Norman Conquest settlements of Flemish people were set in these parts, as elsewhere in England at other times. Hence there is much of interest left to mark a history as stormy and rocky as the coast line. Their milk cans are like no others anywhere else in England—and you'll have to cross the Channel to the Low Countries before you match them! (Yes; and from the time the inhabitants are milk-fed babies they will imbibe subtle differences that continue to breed a people different from all others in England.)

Farther South, the granite cliffs clash down to Land's End (122), and west wind and rain and great Atlantic rollers thunder and roar around their bases. All Cornwall has a rock-bound coast, with hollows that dip steeply to sheltered bathing coves. Hereabouts they will turn you toys out of the rich Cornish serpentine, a green stone veined red, a red stone veined green, or white and crackled and spotted as a moor-bird's egg.

Inland a little are queer white dumpy cliffs and mounds of quarried china clay (124). This makes the streams run like milk in the meadows—white and creamy as new milk. The first time my dog, a sensitive red setter, saw the sight, he "pointed" till he quivered with emotion. "Land of Milk! and NO cats!" then he set to work to lap it up—and I never saw an animal more taken aback! You can use this white water for some few things, but it makes queer tea. Quantities of this clay used to go out to China for dressing silks, and now in addition to its ceramic use the stuff is used to coat paper for illustration printing, as the much debated (but indispensable) "art" paper.

Farther on, in Devon, is a mess of red earth, and broken red cliffs over which the lavender sea-pinks blow, and the scent of the gorse comes down the warm combes to the sheltered sandy bays. Farther east are the Dorset cliffs, and beyond them the beautiful little Lulworth Cove, where the hard cliff line has broken down and left a perfect circular tidal pool. Continuing east there are the Purbeck Hills whose quarries in the Middle Ages furnished the greenish shelly stone which they turned and polished into long slender shafts for many cathedrals and churches. The quarries hereabouts are still some of the most interesting in England.

Beyond the cliffs of the Isle of Wight stand up the white sharp Needles. Then, after levels and shingle reaches, come the Seven Sisters, and the white cliffs of Dover.

Curiously illuminating is the importance of this strip of white cliff landfall. Perhaps, more than anything else, it marks us as an island and maritime nation, *since it is by this one white landfall we are so well known*. . . . "England is called Albion by reason of the white cliffs that are therein."

Less than a third of our English coast line is white! yet— those low white misty cliffs, with the green grass line above and the seas awash below, are the cliffs best loved by many Englishmen who do not live in England. Why? Because they are the last of our land we see on leaving, and the first our straining eyes see on coming Home.

124   CHINA CLAY MINES NEAR ST. AUSTELL, CORNWALL.   The dumps of Spoil spread
white beyond the Workings

125 THE EAST COAST HERRING FLEET FAR AFIELD
AT PLYMOUTH

126 SEA-BOOTS AND FISHING-NETS AT HARTLEPOOL

127 PITCH AND TOSS : Drifters in Rough Weather

128 ATLANTIC BREAKERS ON THE CORNISH COAST

KINGSWEAR AND THE DART ESTUARY AMONG DEVON HILLS

INDEX

(The numerals in italics denote the *figure numbers* of illustrations)

A Selected List of
BATSFORD BOOKS

relating to

Architecture, Fine and Decorative Art, Interior Decoration, Gardens, Social History, Crafts, Applied Science, Engineering, etc.

Published by B. T. BATSFORD LTD

Booksellers and Publishers by Appointment to H.M. The Queen

15 North Audley Street, Mayfair
London, W.1

CONTENTS

NOTE.—This list comprises about 190 books on the subjects shown above from Batsford's main catalogue, in which are listed some 600 odd titles. It is intended to form a representative selection for the use of readers, but those interested in any particular subject should obtain the main catalogue (which will be sent post free on request), that comprises a much wider range of titles under every head. Fully illustrated prospectuses of most books can also be sent on request. Patrons are reminded that Batsford's new premises are at 15 North Audley Street, London, W.1, one minute from Oxford Street, on the main thoroughfare leading to Grosvenor Square, two minutes' walk from either Bond Street or Marble Arch Stations on the Central London Railway; there an immense stock of books, old and new, English and foreign, with prints, pictures, etc., can be inspected at leisure in the large and beautifully-fitted new showrooms. *Telephone Mayfair* 6118 ; *Accounts and Production, Mayfair* 4337. *Cables: Batsfordia, London. Telegrams: Batsford, Audley, London.*

A full index of the books contained in this list, arranged alphabetically under the names of authors, is given on page 32.

List G. 50m. 3/35.